PERFƎCT
IS BORING

PERF∃CT IS BORING

---

10 THINGS MY CRAZY, FIERCE MAMA TAUGHT ME ABOUT BEAUTY, BOOTY, AND BEING A BOSS

TYRA BANKS

AND

CAROLYN LONDON

A TarcherPerigee Book

tarcherperigee

An imprint of Penguin Random House LLC
375 Hudson Street
New York, New York 10014

Most TarcherPerigee books are available at special quantity discounts for bulk purchase for sales promotions, premiums, fund-raising, and educational needs. Special books or book excerpts also can be created to fit specific needs. For details, write: SpecialMarkets@penguinrandomhouse.com.

LIBRARY OF CONGRESS CATALOGING-IN-PUBLICATION DATA
Names: Banks, Tyra, author. | London, Carolyn, author.
Title: Perfect is boring : 10 things my crazy, fierce mama taught me about beauty, booty, and being a boss / Tyra Banks and Carolyn London.
Description: New York : TarcherPerigee, [2018]
Identifiers: LCCN 2017057372 (print) | LCCN 2017059180 (ebook) | ISBN 9780525504290 | ISBN 9780143132301
Subjects: LCSH: Banks, Tyra. | London, Carolyn. | Models (Persons)—United States—Biography. | Self-esteem. | Self-realization. | Success.
Classification: LCC HD8039.M772 (ebook) | LCC HD8039.M772 U5356 2018 (print) | DDC 650.1—dc23
LC record available at https://lccn.loc.gov/2017057372

Printed in the United States of America
1 3 5 7 9 10 8 6 4 2

Book design by Sabrina Bowers

CONTƎNTS

1

INTRODUCTION:

This photo pretty much sums up our whole dynamic:
I'm crazy, but my mama is crazier.

Tyra: Hi, my name is Tyra Banks, and you might remember me from that time I yelled at a girl on TV.

Yeah, you remember that time.

If I was a singer, "Be Quiet, Tiffany" would be my top-of-the-charts number-one-hit-single bat mitzvah dance floor filler that you and your gay best friend cue up every time you go sing karaoke, and you got the GIF saved on your phone, just so it's ready to go the next time someone starts telling you something you don't want to hear.

And you know what? I'm not mad at that, because that moment that's all over the Internet is really just me embodying someone I love so damn much: my mother.

'Cause I ain't crazy, but my mama sure is.

Carolyn: Ty, now when you say "crazy," you mean it in that good way, right? Shoot, girl. I ain't even gonna ask, 'cause I know you do!

Tyra: Well, let me see—do I? When I say that my mama is crazy, what I mean is . . .

Crazy in a letting-your-grandbabies-pull-your-wig-off-and-let-them-wear-it-to-brunch way.

Crazy in an eating-spilled-chili-off-the-dusty-kitchen-floor-cuz-that's-her-famous-recipe-and-it-ain't-gonna-go-to-waste way.

Crazy in an always-got-your-back-even-when-everyone-else-says-you're-down-and-out kinda way.

Crazy in a using-her-juicy-belly-bloops-as-a-musical-instrument way.

Crazy in that tough-love-that-gets-the-point-across-for-real way.

Crazy in a talking-'bout-secretions-on-Amtrak kinda way.

Crazy in a beautiful, talented, loving, and supportive kinda way.

So . . . yes.

You're right, Mama. When I say "crazy," I mean amazing, awesome, incredible, mind-blowing, stupendous.

For me, crazy is good. Crazy is the opposite of boring.

Carolyn: I like that. I ain't been boring a day in my life, so if you wanna call me crazy, I'll take it!

Tyra: I think we can all agree—me and yeah . . . you reading this book right now and Mama—that "Be quiet, Tiffany!" was my craziest moment (it's always number one on any Internet list of "29 Reasons Why TyTy Is One Color Short of a Rainbow" or something like that). It was also the time that all the Mama in me came spewing out, like one of those baking-soda-and-vinegar volcanoes you made for your elementary school science fair (and with my red hair, I kinda looked like a volcano).

So let us just break down all the wig-shaking, finger-pointing, mouth-flapping insanity that spawned a million memes.

Tiffany was a girl on cycle 3 of *America's Next Top Model*. She was so beautiful and talented, with a rags-to-riches story. She didn't make it to the final cast of that cycle, but she had something special about her so we invited her back for a cycle 4 audition and, bam, she made it. On cycle 4, her photos were getting better and better. She was someone who had already been through so much, and I could see where she was going. We invested in her, and she invested in herself. I thought she was going to be the winner. Scratch that—I knew she was gonna be the winner.

Carolyn: Tyra had been raving about Tiffany every time I talked to her. She said that when she saw Tiffany model, she felt like she was looking at the winner of the show. She had never said that—ever.

I was never someone who put tons of emphasis on physical beauty. For me, inner beauty is much more important, and I passed that on to Tyra. So, when she looked at the girls on *Top Model*, she was looking at the whole girl—not just their posing or their runway walks. How they laughed, how they smiled, how they treated other people, how they lit up a room, or their quest, their fire, their journey.

Tyra connected to Tiffany's spirit and her potential. Tiffany was pure heart and soul, and Tyra was set on making sure that beauty rose to where she deserved to be.

Tyra: That cycle, we had created a judging room challenge that had the models doing mock live TV commentating and reading really difficult words off a teleprompter—things in French, difficult designer names, tough technical terms for patterns and stitches. The point wasn't to see who knew how to pronounce the words perfectly, but who could butcher the heck out of them without losing her cool. We knew that no one—no one—was going to get those cray-cray words right. Everyone tried their hardest and everyone messed up, but when Tiffany messed up, we felt like she acted like she personally had been set up to fail. That all the other girls were perfect and she, well, wasn't. Like it was her fate to lose, entirely out of her control.

Something inside me just couldn't take that. I was looking at this beautiful black butterfly who had finally exited her cocoon, and she was pretty much saying that she wasn't good enough to really spread her wings. There have been countless times in my career when I heard that I couldn't do something because I was black, and that only made me want to go out there and prove everyone wrong. Now, to have a girl who had already overcome so much standing in front of me talking about how she couldn't do things because circumstance and fate were in her way, well . . . You saw what happened. (And you might want to turn down the volume, 'cause it's about to get loud.)

BE QUIET, TIFFANY—BE QUIET! WHAT IS WRONG WITH YOU? STOP IT!

I HAVE NEVER IN MY LIFE YELLED AT A GIRL LIKE THIS. WHEN MY MOTHER YELLS LIKE THIS, IT'S BECAUSE SHE LOVES ME.

I WAS ROOTING FOR YOU; WE WERE ALL ROOTING FOR YOU. HOW DARE YOU? LEARN SOMETHING FROM THIS.

WHEN YOU GO TO BED AT NIGHT, YOU LAY THERE AND YOU TAKE RESPONSIBILITY FOR YOURSELF, 'CAUSE NOBODY'S GONNA TAKE RESPONSIBILITY FOR YOU.

YOU ROLLIN' YOUR EYES AND YOU ACTING LIKE THIS BECAUSE YOU'VE HEARD IT ALL BEFORE. YOU'VE HEARD IT ALL BEFORE—YOU DON'T KNOW WHERE THE HELL I COME FROM; YOU HAVE NO IDEA WHAT I'VE BEEN THROUGH.

BUT I'M NOT A VICTIM; I GROW FROM IT, AND I LEARN.

TAKE RESPONSIBILITY FOR YOURSELF.

(I typed that in caps 'cause yeah, I was yellin' like a banshee when I said it.)

I'd been in this banshee situation before, but on the other side. I got one of those real, raw, no-holding-back "Be quiet, Tiffany" diatribes from my mama at least twice a year. Or maybe three times a year. Wait, who am I kidding? It's probably more like four. To this day, whenever she gets tired of hearing me doubt myself, or when she thinks I'm about to give up because something turns out to be a little harder than I expected, she grabs me by the shoulders, shakes me, and screams, "BE QUIET, TYRA!"

Mama was never about just breaking me down. It was always—and still is—about building me up. In that two-minute televised Tyrade, I dropped several truth bombs on Tiffany that were filled with the very lessons that Mama had tried so hard to teach me. Mama always told me that I was beautiful no matter what and that I was worthy no matter what, and that's the message I want to pass on to women and men everywhere. It ain't about me. It's about us. I don't want you getting in your own way as you strive to reach your big, fat, sexy, juicy goals.

Carolyn: I wasn't there on set that day, but Tyra came to my house as soon as production wrapped. I could tell something was up, because she was quieter than usual when she walked in the door.

"Mama, something happened on set today, and . . . I don't know if I should air it."

Something about the way she said this made me realize that she wasn't talking about the standard-issue drama that went down on *Top Model*—someone being super rude at a go-see, a girl writing words on her booty cheeks, or a model cheating on her boyfriend in Milan and crying under a table while getting cursed out by her irate boyfriend back home.

"Ty, what happened?" I asked. "What did you do?"

"I'm just gonna let you watch the tape," she said.

Then she played me the uncut version, and the hair stood up on the back of my neck.

Tyra: When I walked off set that day, my heart was pounding and I had to catch my breath. I knew I had done the right thing (or had I?), but still, there was a part of me that was surprised as hell.

What the eff was that?

I could feel the eyes as I walked back to my trailer. Not on me, but on the ground, as no one on my crew wanted to make eye contact or talk to me. "Tyra has lost her goddamned mind," they were probably all thinking. Probably? Shoot. I'm sure they were sure I needed meds stat.

Had I truly flipped the switch? No one could believe what had just happened. Not even Mama.

Least of all me.

Carolyn: What Tyra showed me was bone-chilling.

Nobody ever believed that Tyra was my daughter. From the time she was born, people asked me if she was adopted—she had this pale skin, these gray eyes, and this sandy reddish hair. Plus, when she grew up, she was almost six feet tall and built like a gazelle with big boobies. I was a human, and my daughter was some alien Amazonian being from that race of people we call "supermodels."

But when I saw that tape of her yelling at Tiffany, it was like I was watching myself.

It was me up there talking to Tiffany.

Everyone's always teased me about how I look when I get upset. My eyes turn into little slits and I talk through my teeth and I point. My. Finger. With. Every. Word. 'Cause I'm tryna drill my message into your brain.

And that's exactly what Tyra was doing.

And everything that was coming out of her mouth was a version of something I'd once said to her.

The apple doesn't fall far from the I-look-crazy-right-now-but-I-swear-I'm-not-I-just-believe-in-you tree.

Tyra: At first, I wasn't sure we should air it. I mean, yes, I have gone far on TV. I've worn a prosthetic suit to expose the harsh judgment of obese people, dressed as a man to show how people responded to rap posses, posed as homeless, and pretended to be a stripper to find out why the heck men are so enthralled with G-strings and pasties in public places, but all of those big moments were produced.

This wasn't.

It was unplanned.

It was raw and real.

It was emotional. Maybe even too much, because it made people uncomfortable.

It was one of the few times in my life that I had lost control, when I cracked and everything came spilling out. People pressure celebrities to be perfect, but this was one of my most flawed moments.

Did I want to put it out there for all the world to see?

I'VE ALWAYS TOLD MY *Top Model* girls that perfect is boring. I got that from my mama (and Eve even said it to Lindsay Lohan's character, Casey, in the cult movie that I starred in, *Life-Size*). But of course, when I said it, I wasn't just talking about looks. I was talking about life.

The only way to live a perfect life is to not take risks, to just sit in a little box and never go after what you want or reach for your goals (because, God forbid, ya could try and ya could fail, and that sho' ain't perfect). When you care a lot about someone or something, you're more likely to do imperfect things. Ya know, like freak out and yell.

So, what was I gonna do?

Try to sweep the imperfections under my Kool-Aid-colored red wig, or air it out, even if it got a little messy?

Well, Mama always taught me not to be afraid of messy.

Even if it was a hot mess.

Carolyn: I thought people *needed* to see this side of Tyra. It showed that she was an emotional human being, and a human being who cared. Sometimes too much.

"I don't know, Ty. I'm thinkin' you need to put this out there,"

I said. "People need to see that you're not some impeccable lil model chick that produces some TV. You are really real. For real."

Tyra: So on the air it went, and the whole world saw the crazy me, the mama bear side of me. I've been misinterpreted a million times when talking about this, but I don't regret airing it. *Top Model* is not just some reality show I do on the side to make some money—it's a platform for me to change lives and the perception of beauty, and this moment just showed how much I care.

I am who I am today because my mama mama'd me (yes, *mama'd* is an official word, as of now) like nothing you've ever seen before. She was a G. She managed the early parts of my modeling career and sacrificed a lot (no, actually, *all*) of her own dreams so that I could make mine come true. Every accolade I get, every accomplishment I've achieved, all my iconic moments and catchy coined phrases (Smize, boo!) are because of her. I am her creation. Her FrankenTy.

Carolyn: My daughter, Tyra, yeah, the supermodel and business mogul (gosh, that sounds awkward to say because, really, she's just my baby girl), is here today and not ummm . . . shall I say, crazy, because of how I parented her. Yeah, she might make up her own words (Ty, I'm your mama, and "pot ledom" still confuses the hell outta me), have some questionable taste in men (child, that "successful" actor didn't have a phone or a car), and Lord, does that girl have gas (she'll clear a room *and* try to blame it on somebody else). But I'm still gonna go ahead and give myself that pat on the back because her accomplishments and spirit—they are honest and pure. Tyra has a good heart, so I guess I must have done something right, right?

Tyra: I decided to write this book with my mama because my story is bananas but even more bananas when people can see that my whole journey is wrapped up in her crazy story, and her crazy story is my crazy story. When my parents got divorced, she moved into a one-bedroom apartment with six-year-old me and my twelve-year-old brother. Within a year, she got us into a two-bedroom. A year after that, we moved into a three. She was a junior-college dropout who got promoted at every job she ever had and held her own in boardrooms with MBAs and CEOs. The only thing Mama ever got handed to her on a plate was some bacon, and even then, I probably came along and took it away because I was worried about her diabetes.

Whether you're a mama or a daughter (or a son or a father—hell, you know we're inclusive over here), I think there's something you can take from our story. Maybe it's how far we've come, how hard we've fought, or how much we've loved, but we hope it inspires you on your own journey.

Besides, Mama and I *had* to do this together—she's the one with the elephant memory, so I'd be calling her seventeen times a day anyway. I might remember we were there, but she remembers what we wore (I had on my bro's air force jacket and a backward baseball cap; she had on her gold hoop earrings and a red cowl-neck sweater), what we ate (barbecue chicken pizza with a basket of gooey garlic bread), and what song was on the radio (Salt-N-Pepa's "Push It").

So now I gotta push it real good. I gotta press rewind and go back to the beginning of Mama's and my story here . . .

Mama was younger than me in this photo, and dang—
she was bangin'!

rrrrrrrrrrrrrrrrrrrrrrrrrrr . . . to when I was born? Nope, a little more . . . *rrrrrrrrrrrrrrrrrrrrrrrrrrrrrrrrrrrrrr* . . . (I'm rewinding a tape here—you remember those? Oh right, you probably don't) . . . *rrrrrrrrrrrrrrrrrrrrrrr*. OK, now that's the spot.

Yep.

So . . .

Press play.

Carolyn London, my crazy, fierce mama, did it—you know, *it* it: knockin' boots, doin' the deed, whatever you want to call it—a whopping (yet entirely underwhelming) 1.5 times as a teenager (more on that later).

The result?

A baby on the way. Luck may not have been on her side, but her fertility was. Poor Mama (I share my own first-time tale later in the book, but you'll have to keep reading to find out where!).

At that time, in 1966, unwed pregnant teenagers were outcast even more than they are today. When she called to try to tell the baby's father, his mother said, "Honey, that's your problem," and hung up the phone. She had a big old pregnant belly, a bouffant hairdo, and the grit of a gladiator. She didn't waste time with the haters; she just had her baby and got on with her life.

Six years later, I came along.

Carolyn: Now, lemme just wipe these tears from my eyes (and the snot from my nose), because I'm always amazed when I'm praised by my baby girl. I'd always wanted a son and a daughter, and when Tyra was born, I grinned like the Cheshire cat (after I got done with all the screamin' and hollerin' in the delivery room, mind you). Little did I know that this tiny girl clinging to my belly would one day have a brain like a Jamba

Mama and me when I was just two.

The three of us lived in a one-bedroom apartment, and Mama worked
her butt off to get us to a two-bedroom and, later, a three.

Juice–whirling blender with no off button, or a NASA rocket ship slicing through the stratosphere to discover places unknown.

I realized one day that the White Rabbit in *Alice's Adventures in Wonderland* ain't got nothing on Miss Tyra. You see, she's also never late for a very important date. Or should I say date, after date, after date. Her calendar of life is always full to the brim, and like the White Rabbit, she's always constantly checking her watch and running from one unimaginable idea to another. She's also got a bit of the Mad Hatter thrown in, and her top hat is that ever-changing crown of weaved hair that I do believe is sewn in so tight that it stimulates the essence of her slew of creative madness. My child still calls me in the middle of the night just to share new ideas that spontaneously popped into her head. ("Mama, I got this show idea I wanna do about models!") And the even crazier thing? So many of her Mad Hatter ideas have actually worked.

👁 👁 *Tyra:* There's all kinds of mamas out there. We're about to break a few down:

There are mothers who expect absolute perfection from their children 24-7. They're strict and stern with lists of rules as long as Steph Curry's three-pointer. Those it's-either-my-way-or-the-highway-so-shut-the-hell-up-because-I-said-so mamas. The ones who seem to have slipped themselves a little pill called Momnesia and don't remember a damn thing about being a rebellious teenager who snuck out of her bedroom window to be with that wild boy who couldn't care less about her except for getting some you-know-what and her parents insisted she stay the heck away from him because he had a . . . well . . . a . . . penis but she still snuck out the window every time that boy called the house and let the phone ring once and then hung up—the secret signal that meant

Tyra and I were as close as can be. But BFFs who hang in the club?
Nah, I'm not that kinda mama.

"I'm coming now, baby, so get ready to jump out that window," and she jumped every damn time. You know those kinds of mothers. We all do. Maybe you even had one. Maybe you are one. You know . . . used to be all loco but now you pretend you were a teenage angel. And I'm not talkin' the Victoria's Secret kind.

My mama . . . naw . . . she wasn't like that.

Carolyn: Nor was I one of those moms who are their child's best friend. You've seen them. Hangin' out big-time with their child. They hit the club with their daughter in the tightest bodycon dress (hello Herve Leger bandage) 'cause that night, Justin Bieber's crew is rumored to be buying shots for everyone who can twerk their butts the hardest and fastest. And they'll sashay together down that morning walk-of-shame runway while sharing the too-juicy details of their sexual conquests with JB's DJ's daddy and his bodyguard's brother's barber.

SMDH.

I was never a hot mess mama. Hold on too tightly and the kids rebel; hold on too loosely and all things go to hell.

Tyra: She tried to be somewhere in the middle of the JB and the yank (yo' butt if you broke her rules).

If you compare my mama to art, she would be modern street art, like my mystery boy, Banksy. (Do you know who Banksy really is? All I'm saying is *Banksy Art* is an anagram of my first and last names. . . . Hold up a sec while I wipe this purple paint from my fingers.) But back to my—I mean Banksy's art . . . Familiar visuals, yet off-kilter and loaded with social commentary on how messed up we all are and how we can make it better with spray-painted figures on the side of some random building. If my mom's style was a cuisine, she'd be molecular gastronomy—foodstuff you know but it comes to the table all unique; smoking, foaming dishes listed on the menu in quotes and full of liquid nitrogen. You kind of freak out at first, but then you put it in your mouth and realize it might actually be one of the best things you've tasted and experienced friggin' ever! (Hey, Chef Achatz!)

Mama could be so raw and real that I'd be squirming in my seat, hoping that lightning would come and strike me upside the head because I was sure that'd be less painful than sitting there listening to her talk like that. She could also be as tough as Gordon Ramsay, but what she was always trying to drill in my thick fivehead was some serious self-esteem.

Carolyn: Most of those talks worked. (And the ones that didn't? Oh, we spill the beans all up in this book, baby, so you don't make the what-the-hell-was-she-thinking mistakes Mizz TyTy did.)

If Tyra were an instrument, she'd be a trumpet—full of energy and hitting all the high notes, but just as capable of turning on the soul and bringing a tear to your eye. One moment she's a fairy godmother, playing the wise character, inspiring and motivating to make dreams come true, and the next, she's my little girl again, sitting on the sofa in our living room eating five flavors of ice cream while watching old DVDs of *Pee-wee's Playhouse*. If she were a dance move, she'd be the Nae Nae, with one hand up and one hand down, just swaying all over the place. If she were an emoji, no doubt she'd be the 😜. (In fact, she's making that face at me right now.)

Tyra likes to make up these silly rap songs, so one day I thought I would compose one about her. Cue the beats.

> *Daughter, oh daughter, oh daughter of mine*
> *Here's my verse, Imma try to make it rhyme.*
> *You're better with age, like my fave port wine.*
> *Guess I done my job, 'cause you turned out fine.*
> *Daughter, oh daughter, oh daughter of mine*
> *Big forehead, with a genius mind*
> *You a mama now, that's so sublime.*
> *You like my mama too, Freaky Friday time.*
> *Daughter, oh daughter, oh daughter of mine.*
> *You make me proud, 'cause you taught me how to rhyme.*
> *My mark on you'll stand the test of time.*
> *Your fierce life's your legacy, when I've left mine.*

👁 👁 *Tyra:* Wow, Mama, now I'm about to cry! But that, ladies and gents, is l-o-v-e. And I've been tryna pass some of that on in my whole career, in every little thing I do.

To you.

When I pulled a Mama up there with Tiffany and let the honesty rip, I wasn't thinking about ratings; I wasn't thinking about it going down in history as one of the most memorable moments on TV; I wasn't thinking about people running up to me on the street a decade later, asking for a selfie and maybe, please if I wouldn't mind, could I just be so nice as to yell at them, too?

I was just thinking about Tiffany, and all those times I'd been standing there in her shoes, doubting myself, feeling like I might just give up and how Mama would have given me a verbal smack upside the head to snap me out of it.

I think of Tiffany often and still have so much love for her. (Every once in a while, a *Top Model* girl in cycles I shoot today reminds me of her, too.) Tiffany was lovable and charismatic; people were always drawn to her, and the other girls enjoyed her. She was tough, but also fun and feisty, with a mouth on her that was always making people laugh and trying to cheer them up (even right up till the end, when she got eliminated).

She's a strong, smart, beautiful woman, and I know from reading recent interviews with her that she's introspective to this day, mature. She gets it. That's rare.

I'm still rooting for her. We're all still rooting for her. And I think now she's rooting for herself, too.

So you know what I do when someone says, "Tyra, my name's Randall/Amanda/Chantel/Brian, and if you could just yell, 'BE QUIET, RANDALL/AMANDA/CHANTEL/BRIAN,' you would make my year!"? I put my rage face on and I wait for them to press record and say go, and then I look right at 'em and belt out, "BE QUIET, RANDALL/AMANDA/CHANTEL/BRIAN!"

And I do it with a smile, because I am not embarrassed about that moment. It was real, raw, heartfelt, and crazy. And not perfect.

Just like my mama.

Just like me.

And just like you.

(Yeah, I called you crazy. You had to know that was coming, right?)

PARENTAL ADVISORY— EXPLICIT CONTENT AHEAD!

Now, I'm not tryna have you write to our publisher about how you wanna go back in time and stage a mass book-burning extravaganza, or set you up to leave all kinds of comments on my Instagram because my mama and I got dirty mouths! So go ahead and put this book in the trash stat (and unfollow me while you're at it) if you get embarrassed or squeamish easily, because we wrote this book for mothers and daughters and fathers and sons everywhere who aren't afraid to tell it like it is. In other words, the lewd, crude, and shrewd—but never the rude! On second thought, this book might be just what you need, boo. (Remember, sometimes it takes a moment to recognize that something is actually exactly what you need; what you want and what you need aren't exactly the same thing.) That said, if you are looking for any or all of the following, then consider a word of warning before you sit back and enjoy this ride:

- ➤ If ya mama never shared anything crass with you, get ready, child! This book is for you!

- ➤ If she shared a lot, be prepared to say amen a million and one times. You know how it is.

- ➤ If you're prudish, keep reading—you will get turnt out, boo!

- ➤ If you got a daughter of your own and you're wondering how to talk to her about all the down-and-dirty, read on!

- ➤ If you wanna laugh your ass off—you got it, honey. Coming your way.

- ➤ If you want to learn how to embrace your booty and tell the world to kiss your fat ass, you've come to the right place.

- ➤ If you want to see what happens when yo mama practices tough love but never lets you down, we got you.

- ➤ If you want to see all the fabulous things that happen when you take control of your destiny, we got you.

2

TAKE RESPONSIBILITY FOR YOURSELF

👁 👁 *Tyra:* When Paris came calling for me in the form of a French modeling angel—well, agent—by the name of Veronique, no one saw it coming. Not my local Los Angeles agency: "Little catalog Tyra?" they said. "That Tyra—who models on weekends and after school? The one we don't really see as making a career of this. You want *her* to go to Paris?"

Not my mama: "What the hell are you talkin' about?" she said, scowling into the phone when the agency called to talk to her.

And certainly not me.

But Veronique said yes, she wanted *me* to go to Paris and model. Well, she said *oui*. And she added that out of all the girls on the board, I was the only model they wanted at her French agency, City Models. She believed I could do quite well in the land of Coco, cafés, and croissants.

Well, hell—nobody knew what to say.

Because I had other plans. Big plans. That began with a *c* and did not involve Coco, cafés, or croissants.

👄 *Carolyn:* I was very excited for Tyra to go to college, because it was an opportunity that I never had. When she first started modeling in high school, she thought catwalking and posing was just going be a side thing, since she knew for sure she was going to a university to study film and television production. Her modeling jobs were a way to help her father and me afford tuition.

I had heard so many negative things about the modeling industry, especially when models were traveling far from home—from girls getting taken advantage of on the other side of the world by photographers who abused their power, to models getting strung out, losing their careers, and getting shipped home. I also just wanted Tyra to have something that was more stable and solid. A career in modeling was so fleeting, and I couldn't imagine my daughter having a life in a field that was all about sitting there and waiting for the damn phone to ring.

Sure, my baby had some beauty, but I was bettin' on her brain.

Tyra: I was so excited for college. I genuinely, truly, honestly, not-just-saying-this-for-the-benefit-of-all-the-grown-ups-in-the-room loved learning. And college was learning with an endgame: studying intensely what you were interested in so that you could prepare for a career that you (hopefully) loved.

So when Veronique insisted I come to Paris, I can honestly say it was something I'd never even thought about. I'd spent the past year dreaming of classrooms and campus quads, not runways and modeling squads. College wasn't just a dream, either. I'd put in work weighing my options and making plans—I'm talking hand-drawn charts and spreadsheets and pros-and-cons lists that stretched from the kitchen all the way down the hall into my bedroom and up against the closet.

At first, the options seemed endless. I'd flip through a college brochure, in my head singing Ariel's "wish I could be . . . part of your world." This was the university for me! Then another brochure would come in the mail and I'd repeat the process because, no, this school—this one was where I truly belonged! Finally, I started to narrow it down. I toured campuses, met with professors, and even checked out the dorms, imagining what color sheets I'd get for the ultralong narrow twin bed and what posters I was gonna put up on the wall (Vanessa Williams, Bell Biv DeVoe, Al B. Sure, En Vogue, DJ Jazzy Jeff & the Fresh Prince?).

I broke down the schools:

UCLA? Close to home and in my fave hangout hood, Westwood, but that student body was *huge.*

Columbia? Ivy League . . . yikes!

NYU? The thrill of New York was tantalizing, but the idea of having to cross a busy city street while dodging taxis to get to class was terrifying.

That's why I fell in love with Loyola Marymount University. The campus was on a hill overlooking the ocean; it was quaint and serene, and the boys on the basketball team were fine as hell (scratch that Will Smith poster that was going on the wall—maybe I'd just become a college b-ball fan). I became smitten with the film and television program at Loyola, and imagined that going to school there would be like getting shot out of a cannon and landing right in the middle of my dream entertainment industry and creating magic behind the camera. On the orientation tour with my dad, I even bought out the student store, taking home the college logo sweatshirts, T-shirts, mugs, key chains, banners, you name it. I had that college student just-woke-up-now-where's-the-dining-hall Smize down.

I was ready, and everyone knew it.

So when Veronique reached out to my agents in Los Angeles about me, they couldn't believe it. They knew how focused I was on going to college, so they hadn't even tried to push me. And honestly, I believe they thought I was just a catalog girl, not high-fashion material. They saw me modeling parkas for Burlington

Coat Factory (you know, the kind with the faux fur hoods where you can't even see your face?) and some cotton nightgowns for Sears (nothing says s-e-x-y like long sleeves and ruffles, amirite?), not sharp-shouldered Saint Laurent blazers or feminine, pink, poufy-sleeved Oscar de la Renta couture gowns.

But I had to admit: Thinking about going to Paris was thrilling. I could see myself up on the runway, but what if the L.A. agency was right?

That thought terrified me, and I spent many nights with my eyes wide open, staring at the ceiling at three a.m.

What if I went and just fell on my face?

What if I came home a failure, and college was just . . . gone?

Carolyn: Tyra wanted to do both. She wanted to go to Paris and go to college, and she kept asking me what she should do. I thought about my own life and how I'd wanted to be a dancer but kept trying to be a secretary because my parents thought that good people grew up to get jobs with the city. It was part of that whole "doin' what a perfect daughter does" thing.

I gave up on dancing, but I never forgot about it, and I never extinguished my dream. Every year, I took Tyra and Devin to see the Alvin Ailey American Dance Theater and the Dance Theatre of Harlem, and I'd watch those dancers with a heavy heart, imagining myself up there, gliding across the stage with them. Maybe I could have been the Misty Copeland or Judith Jamison of my time. Or a Rockette. (Or maybe I should just try out for *America's Got Talent* now. I do have an in. . . .)

I had dreams, but the idea of perfection personified by my parents squashed those dreams flatter than a French crepe. I didn't want to do that to Tyra, so I sat back and told her,

Even though I gave up my dream, I never lost my love for dancing.

"The choice is yours, and I'll support you whatever you decide to do."

👁 👁 *Tyra:* Whatever I decide to do? *Aaauughhhh!*
This was hard as hell to decide. And there was the issue of money. I had made some modeling money, but even with that supplement, college tuition was still going to be a big stretch for my parents. If I could pad my pockets by going to Paris, that could make paying for college a little easier. . . .

Finally, I said ooh-la-la and what the hell, I'll go to Paris.

The decision got a lot easier when Loyola told me I could defer my admission for a year. If Paris was a bust, I'd just end up right back where I started: in film school. So, the worst thing that could happen to me could end up being the best anyway. Yeah, Ma had let me know the decision was mine to make, but also that it wasn't one I should take lightly. That it was called the modeling business, not modeling playtime. College or no, I was still gonna have to study up for Paris.

But first, I was gonna have to tell my Superexcited-his-daughter-got-into-every-college-she-applied-to-Loyola-sweatshirt-wearing Daddy.

Yeah, that's his legal name.

Carolyn: Now, Tyra's daddy adores his baby girl, but did that mean he was gonna support her no matter what she decided to do?

My proud daddy and me at my high school graduation. Three short months later, I had to break the news that instead of going to college, I was going to Paris. Eek!

Tyra: Boy oh boy, was I nervous. My dad was in papa heaven when he had flown me across the country to visit colleges, so having to inform him that I was now Tyra I'm-just-putting-college-off-for-a-year-to-go-to-Paris-to-try-to-model-internationally Banks wasn't easy. (Yes, that was *my* legal name.)

Ma and I took him to dinner at M&M Soul Food in Inglewood. We knew that filling his belly with rich smothered chicken, gooey macaroni and cheese, and collard greens bursting with ham hocks would help him swallow the news with a lot more ease. I mean, hey, the way to a man's change-of-college-plans heart . . .

Carolyn: It worked. He took the news in stride and even ordered peach cobbler for dessert. I was shocked. But, hey . . . never doubt the power of gravy, cheddar, and grease.

Tyra: I was so happy. Amazed, but happy. My dad totally understood that I had a rare opportunity in front of me—a chance to experience the other side of the world, and not as a tourist. Yes, it would be new, scary, and out of my element, but he trusted me. He knew his daughter was no fool.

Carolyn: As I was leaving the parking lot with all three of us in the car, I saw his eyes shift.

Tyra: We needed to make a left-hand turn to take Dad back to his house. As Ma stopped at the intersection, and in the middle of a four-lane street with cars zooming around us everywhere, my dad threw open the passenger door and bolted out of my mom's Honda Accord! I have no idea where he went. He just disappeared into the night.

And he didn't really talk to me for six months.

Crap. Maybe all that gravy didn't sit well?

Carolyn: Seeing her daddy bolt into the dark didn't make Tyra change her mind. I think it just made her more determined not to fail because she didn't want to let him down. I told her that she was not leaving Los Angeles until she had learned everything she possibly could about the French fashion industry. "If all you can tell me is that they eat lots of croissants and have sexy accents and that the top fashion house is Chanel, you are staying your butt in L.A. because you will fail in Paris," I said. "And you are not gonna fail." And so she began her I-will-not-fail-Paris crash course.

Tyra: I had two weeks, and lemme tell you, this was before you could just whip out your cell phone while standing in line for the bathroom at JCPenney and Google "everything I need to know about French fashion." I had to work. I had to use books. I had to look things up on paper. *Gasp!*

Cue the preparation montage!

Ty minus 14 days: I hit the fashion library in downtown L.A., and I hit it hard. Because Mama was a photographer, she'd always read fashion magazines sideways so that she could read the photographers' names, which, in those days, were listed in tiny type in the gutter. At the fashion library, the librarian told me that was where I should also look for the names of everyone else who had worked on the shoot: the editors, stylists, makeup artists, hairdressers. My aha moment was when I realized that in the top magazines, they were usually the same damn names! I ran home and told Ma right away. She smiled. "Then it looks like those are the people you should strive to work for," she said.

Ty minus 10 days: Time to find the remote and turn on the TV. We popped some popcorn and started taking notes on CNN's *Style with Elsa Klensch* and MTV's *House of Style* with Cindy Crawford. I checked out VHS archives of all the biggest Paris Fashion Week shows and practically broke the tapes hitting rewind. Mama and I watched everything from the biggest name— Chanel—to the most obscure—Lolita Lempicka—and I was glued to the screen watching the models strut down the runway. I saw that all the best girls had a little signature thing they'd do—whether it was the way they moved their eyes, a pirouette at the end, or a bold stompin' step—that made them stand out from everyone else. I got to where I could identify a model just by her sashay in the dark in silhouette. Yasmeen Ghauri had the tiniest waist, and every step looked like she was dislocating a hip. Sounds crazy but she was *fierce*! Marpessa's hips swayed, but she was lithe and light with a slight smile on her face. Sonia Cole took off a coat and gloves on the catwalk like David friggin' Blaine. Pure friggin' fierce magic!

Ty minus 7 days: Oh my God, I need a signature walk!

Ty minus 6 days: Mom tossed me her highest heels and draped the longest silk nightgown she owned over my shoulders. It was salmon colored and divine! Sometimes we'd throw a bathrobe over it to simulate an overcoat or tie a king-size sheet to my waist to pretend it was a train on a couture gown. Mama was a genius with those linen closet creations. Squint and you almost believed they were one-of-a-kind Dior couture that could cause tripping problems if you didn't know what the heck you were doing. I'd walk back and forth, down the hallway and across the living room, as she sat on the couch with her ginger ale.

Ty minus 5 days: Mama gave me feedback on—a.k.a. criticized the hell outta—my walk. "Ty, you're pooching out your lips while you walk. Your lips are already full and beautiful, so stop that," she'd say.

"But Mama, I feel fierce when I push my lips out." Fierce. I loved that word and was using it more and more often, because it always felt like the word I was searching for: sexy, but powerful with a lil wink on the side.

I'd try again.

"Still poochin'," Mama would say. I'd head back to the hallway and prepare to do it again.

Ty minus 4 days: "Tyra, you're bouncing a lot—too much. Reel it in."

"But Mama, I feel fierce when I bounce a lot. I think it could be my signature."

"All right, then hone that bounce so you're in control of it and your boobies don't jiggle all over the place."

"Like this, Mama?"

"Yep. So much better." And then she'd sing, "Less bounce, to the ounce," to the tune of Zapp & Roger's tune.

Ty minus 3 days: I knew I got it when I sashayed across that living room floor and Mama jumped up off the couch and yelled, "Yes, girl! *FIERCE!*"

Ty minus 2 days: Hair and makeup prep.

When I watched the fashion shows, I didn't just watch the walks. I also paid attention to each model's hair and makeup to see what kind of glam and girl each designer looked for. Yves Saint Laurent wanted girls who looked like bitchy ballerinas, with slicked-back buns and bold, red lips. Chanel wanted twirly-pearls girls, with big hair and joie de vivre smiles even in their quilted power suits. I had to learn to quickly create these looks myself so that I could walk into castings looking like the spitting image of each designer's ideal girl. Red lipstick, check. Bobby pins, check. Hair grease, check. Powder, check. Scarf, check. . . .

Ty minus 1 day: If . . . I . . . can . . . just . . . get . . . this . . . gosh . . . darned . . . suitcase . . . closed. "Mama, come sit on this for me!"

Liftoff:

Daddy had been giving me the silent treatment, but he broke it long enough to come with Mama to take me to LAX so I could catch my flight to Paris. I was bawling as

I walked through the terminal to get on that plane. Snot, boogers, tears . . . the ugliest KKW cry you can imagine. I kept facing forward as I walked away from them and tried to put as much pep in my step as I could. I did not want my dad to see my contorted face and panic. And I did not want my mom to know I was scared out of my mind. Gosh, I wanted to turn around and give one last look. One last good-bye. But I didn't want to crush my parents. So instead I put my hand high in the air and waved to them . . .

. . . without looking back.

Carolyn: She had a signature walk, and she knew who the power players were. She had an arsenal of quick-change looks, enough for James Bond or some international spy, so she could transform instantly for each go-see. You weren't just a model on that catwalk; you were a silent-movie actress. And the runway wasn't just a walk; it was an audition. You had a goal: stand out on the runway and end up in the magazines. And if you're lucky, your face stares back at millions from the cover. Tyra was a black girl, so we knew covers were not a real possibility, but it didn't matter. She was ready for Paris. And we put all of this together in our living room.

At the airport that day, her daddy and I didn't take our eyes off of her as she walked away from us toward her plane until she disappeared in the crowd.

The one thing I don't understand to this day is why she didn't turn back to give us one last good-bye.

👁 👁 *Tyra:* If I had any fantasies about modeling being nonstop glamour and sophistication, those died as soon as I got on the plane. My seat number was something like 72E, and I was in a middle seat right by the bathrooms. I had to fold my giraffe legs up underneath me like a flamingo or else my knees were jammed up against the seat in front of me, and every time the bathroom door opened, I started gaggin' and reachin' for my barf bag. There was a line of people right by my seat, all sweating and anxious about getting into that bathroom so that they could take an after-dinner poop. The only thing that covered up the eau de poo-poo was the cigarette smoke from the dozens of people who lit butt after butt the entire eleven hours it took to get to Paris. By the time the flight landed at Charles de Gaulle, I was gasping for a breath that I never had a second to catch.

I had never been anyplace where people didn't speak English— oh wait, I'm an L.A. girl and made a few family trips to Tijuana, Mexico, but Europe and passports and airplanes, oh my! Nor had I ever traveled without chaperones, but I had to swallow my fear about being in a strange land full of only strangers, because as soon as I was off that plane, it was on.

I hailed a taxi, which I had never done before, and went straight to the modeling agency. Mama had bought me a currency calculator, but shoot, it wasn't a translator, so when my ride ended and it was time to pay, I nervously held out a handful of francs and let the cabdriver take what he needed. "You better not be ripping me off," I said, in English he didn't understand.

"French French French French," he said back, in French that I did not understand. Oh well, I thought, at least I took one taxi right without getting abducted.

So far, Paris was a success.

My new agent, Veronique, wanted me to come straight to their office, so there I was in front of the wrought iron gates of the City

Models agency building at 22 Rue Jean Mermoz when the taxi pulled away. "Hello?" I called out, loudly through the gates. "Bonjour?" I tried, softer. Finally, someone buzzed me in, but I still had to drag all my suitcases up two flights of stairs by myself; the elevator was not working. When I found the office, I was sweating and my foot was throbbing from where I'd dropped my suitcase—with no wheels; ones with wheels didn't exist yet if you weren't a flight attendant—on my toe.

If I was expecting a café au lait and a "How was your trip?" I did not get it. The office was full of people in black, smoking and yelling into a million different phones and speaking English with accents as thick as a slice of Cheesecake Factory cheesecake. Someone thrust some papers into my hands. "You have fifteen go-sees," she said.

"Great!" I said. "I'll just go drop my suitcases off at the models' apartment and after a shower and a good night's sleep—"

"Non non non non non," she said. "Now. Get orange card and phone card, and you go now." Then she practically kicked my butt back down those stairs that I'd just dragged myself up.

You needed a phone card to use the pay phones (yep, no portable cell phones existed back then) and an orange card to ride the subway (Uber what?). I got the phone card no problem, but the orange card was proving a little difficult. "Hi, ma'am. Um . . . I need to buy an orange card," I said to the woman behind the counter. I got back a withering stare and a flurry of French.

I tried again. "Orange card? For the um . . . the subway."

Same. But this time with a roll of her blue-eyeshadowed eyes.

"Orange card. Like, uh . . . I really need an orange card." A line was forming behind me, and I looked around desperately for a dropped card on the ground that I could maybe just point at.

"Oh-runnngh card?" she said back to me, and shrugged like

Tyra's Carte Orange from Paris.

she had no idea what I was talking about. I was just about to panic when someone tapped me on the shoulder.

"Excusez-moi, mademoiselle," he said. "But you must try to speak the French. French people are so nice when you try to speak the French."

Oh. I nodded eagerly. I could do that. "Thank you," I said to him. "How do I say 'orange card'?"

"Carte Orange." My jaw musta dropped. Seriously, what the . . . That was it? That lady knew what the heck I was saying! Whatever. I turned back to her at the counter.

"Carte Orange?" I said sheepishly, followed by "See voo play." She sprang to life.

"Ah! Carte Orange!" She smiled as she took my money and slid the orange card out to me. Then she said, "Welcome to beautiful Paris, young American girl!" with hardly any accent.

She showed my ass that I needed to respect where the heck my ass was.

Damn. Her lesson stuck. To this day I always try to speak as much of the native tongue of the land I am in. But anyway . . .

I was on my way. And ready to slay the day. (That rhymes.)

With my Carte-freaking-Orange, I got around that city's arrondissements (little towns all over the city; there's twenty of them) like I was born in Paris. Before I'd walk into castings, I'd duck into doorways and do my hair and makeup according to what I knew that designer liked. Lots of the other models would breeze into castings in high-heeled Michel Perry boots and sleek new outfits they'd bought in Milan (and they looked damn good), but I didn't think twice about showing up in my baggy jeans, Timberlands, and my high school backpack with my portfolio inside. I felt that if my hair and makeup looked on theme, it wasn't about how I looked in my clothes.

It was about how I looked in *their* clothes.

Every time I walked into a casting, I would walk that designer's style with the glam look he or she adored (I was obsessed with playing the part of their signature girl) and was usually asked to then try on an outfit. Contrary to what you see on TV on my dear *America's Next Top Model* and those go-sees I send the girls on, design houses don't always ask you to try on their clothes. I felt so on point looking the part and walking the part. And the VHS tapes that my mom and I had studied burned brightly in my head from casting to casting.

My first week in Paris, I met a fine-ass male model named Paul at one of my castings. He was black, had this weird yet glorious kind of beauty that was just my style, and he was British. Lord, that accent was like butter melting on some hot sourdough bread. When he asked for my number, I was intrigued but terrified. I was used to boys, but this was a M-A-N. So what'd I do? I flat-out refused, even though I shared a phone with other girls in the models' apartment and probably would have never gotten the message that he'd called anyway.

In all my time in Paris, I never dated any models. I didn't date any nonmodels either. Flat out, I didn't date. Lots of girls were getting busy on the reg with all the French and otherworldly fineness that surrounded us, but I was all about that biz, baby.

Which was great for my career (no distractions!) but also meant I was alone. A lot.

Fashion fittings would go until midnight at times, so getting home on the subway was kinda scary, and I wasn't making taxi money yet. Plus, early on, I hardly knew the streets (they call them *rues*) and could barely speak the language. And remember, there were no cell phones!

So I created something special. My "lunatic walk."

I'd come up the stairs from the subway, then start talking to myself. "Well, all them green aliens they just come down and take my Cover Girl mascara juice and Jesus said thou shalt have fried schrimps and radioactive ice cream . . . Chanel Saint Laurent, shut cho ass up! I will burn you!" I'd shout, spin around in circles, and box the air like I was punching something only I could see.

Any potential predators would take one look at me and think, "Huh, well, I ain't *#¥$ing with that crazy chick." (They'd think that in French, of course.)

I did it every single night and even taught it to a few of the other models as well. "If you have to walk these midnight Paris streets by yourself," I'd say, "just act friggin' bonkers. No one's going to mess with yo buck-wild ass."

THE ESSENTIAL TRAITS OF A
KICK-ASS LUNATIC WALK

1. The gaze: It should be off in the distance. If someone tries to talk to you, never make eye contact. Pretend they got a parrot on their shoulder, and look at the parrot.

2. The punches: Unseen enemies come at ya from all sides. Throw some left hooks, some right jabs, some crosses to the side, some uppercuts while spinning around. For extra credit, some kickboxing kicks will up the ante.

3. The stroll: Never walk in a straight line. Zig, zag, stumble, and stutter-step.

4. The voice: Sometimes you're yelling, sometimes you're whispering, but you never stop talking to yourself. Throw in some threatening words every once in a while.

5. The body: Your head twitches, your arms twitch, your knees twitch. Everything is moving all the time.

6. Get home safely.

Carolyn: So a seventeen-year-old girl gets on a plane and goes to Paris and goes to audition after audition. They ask her to put on their clothes and walk. So she does. Their mouths fall open.

She books twenty-five shows in her first season.

Tyra: Twenty-five fashion shows. Magazine spreads up the yin-yang. The agents at City Models let me know this was standard. No biggie.

Carolyn: The agency told me twenty-five fashion shows and Tyra's success was phenomenal and that most girls were lucky to book three shows. She was doing so well that the agency started to get scared that her head was gonna blow up like a hot air balloon, and they were calling me so much that I was starting to get in trouble at my job because my phone was ringing off the hook.

"Hello, this is Carolyn," I'd answer.

"You must not tell 'er!" someone would scream at me through the phone, French accent crackling the wires all the way across the Atlantic as I practically dropped the receiver. "Tee-rah is such nice girl and *elle* must not know! We do not want her to *changement*! Tee-rah is so grounded! So *normale*! We want to keep 'er zat way!"

When I talked to Tyra, I would try to keep the excitement out of my voice. "That's great, Ty," I'd tell her when she related a story about how his reps pulled Yves Saint Laurent himself out of the back room so that he could see Tyra in person. "The agency said you're doing just fine."

Just pondering in Paris: on a break from a photo shoot,
wondering if I made the right decision to come.

Tyra: "Did you book any shows?" my room-
mate at the models' apartment would ask me.

"Oh yeah," I'd say, lacing up my Tims. "Today I have Dior,
YSL, and Chanel. Karl Lagerfeld has requested to have me come
early so he can spend more time figuring out my looks. You
wanna ride the Métro to Karl together?"

I didn't understand—I thought it was like sharing notes in
chemistry class or talking about what book you were gonna read
for the book report. Instead, I was looking like a braggadocious
bee-yotch.

Touch-ups backstage in Paris
at the Lolita Lempicka fashion show.

But damn, I kept being told I was doing average and that all the new girls were doing this.

Carolyn: Tyra even booked the covers of two French magazines, one called *20 Ans*, which is like *Seventeen*, and one called *Jeune et Jolie*, which means "young and happy" and is like the French *Glamour*. That was a shock for almost everybody, because back in the United States, no one was talking about putting a new black girl on the cover of anything!

Tyra: I only finally started to guess what was up toward the end of the season, when camera crews would bum-rush me backstage at shows, jabbing microphones in my face. "You are zee new girl. How does it feel to be zee new it girl, Tee-rah?"

It girl?

Say what?

I was still just tryna perfect my midnight lunatic walk and also stay focused in the daytime so I didn't end up with regrets about not going to college.

Carolyn: I was shocked when the agency offered to pay for me to fly to Paris to break the news of her success to Tyra (though I still wonder today if they took it outta her check as

Signing autographs after the shows in Paris. At the time, I had no idea why anyone wanted my autograph. Looking back, I have no idea why I'm holding a wig!

46

"expenses"), but I said yes immediately! Then I hopped on a plane and flew eleven hours so that I could stop lying to my daughter and tell her that she was a hit.

Ty met me at the airport, screaming, "Mommy! Mommy!" and waving her arm off. We hadn't seen each other in so long and were hugging and crying, making a big, loud, corny American tourist scene that made everybody stare.

Tyra: And Mama was impressed because my French was poppin'!

Carolyn: It was! Somehow, even with all that fashion craziness, Tyra had found the time and headspace to learn French! I couldn't believe it when we got in a taxi and she was giving the driver directions like she'd been born with escargot in her mouth. She knew the city, she knew the language, and she was lightin' up the City of Light!

Tyra: I'd come a long way from, "Um, can I have an orange card?"

Carolyn: Even more, she knew the industry! Rocking my high heels and bedsheets, reading magazines sideways, watching runway VHS tapes till they started to flicker, and having a makeover spy kit in her backpack paid off, big-time.

Was I surprised?

Nah, baby.

Yes, it was her time for Paris. It was her moment. Sprinkled with a dash of luck.

LEFT: Mama and me *werking* it backstage at the Claude Montana show in Paris when I was eighteen.

BELOW: Mama was my backstage cheerleader and protector in the early days (not all the other models were happy to see a newcomer so successful). This was also one of my fave makeup looks EVER!

But without all of that crazy preparation, that moment would have flown past her like a cab in NYC not stopping for a brotha'man who's headed uptown after five p.m. All she woulda felt was the breeze of opportunity passing her by.

So, no. I wasn't surprised.

Not.

One.

Bit.

👁 👁 *Tyra:* Mama broke the news to me as gently as she could.

I hadn't just survived my first season in Paris; I'd kicked its freakin' butt. As amazing as this was, it brought a new dilemma. Since I had just deferred my admission to Loyola, it was still a dream that I could peek out the window and wave at occasionally, like a camp friend you lose touch with but don't worry about 'cause you know you'll see her again next summer and you'll go right back to being BFFs.

To officially say I wasn't going to college meant cutting that cord, and closing the door on my TV-producing dreams.

On the flip, modeling wouldn't wait. I had a chance to be successful, do more than just pad my college fund, and build a real and legit career in fashion. If I blinked or even hesitated, that might just evaporate right in front of my eyes.

"Mama, what do I do?!" I wanted her to tell me what to do, to take the whole thing off my shoulders and make the decision easier, but as usual, she just sat there, this time flipping through a copy of *Vogue Paris*, turning the fashion spreads sideways so that she could locate the photographer's name like she had all the time and not a care in the world. "Ty, baby"—flip, flip—"you know I ain't gonna tell you what to do." Flip.

So I made the choice (you know what I chose) and kept sleeping in my LMU sweatshirt every night.

Choosing to model meant I wasn't going to college, but it didn't mean I had to stop learning. In fact, it was the opposite. I wasn't in a classroom, but modeling was a nonstop education and I soaked it up every which way. Cab rides were my French class. Runway shows were theater. Interviews were public speaking. Contract negotiations were business. Living in the model housing was sociology (and a little bit of social work). And for art history, Paris Fashion Week took place at the Louvre. (They have this little painting there, maybe you've heard of it? It's called the *Mona Lisa.* . . .)

Seventeen years old, saluting the city with my portfolio in my high school backpack!

I hit the ground running in my Timberlands in Paris because I had taken the time to prepare, and that is a tactic that I've stuck with my entire career. I never just assume that someone is going to come along and tell me everything I need to know, and you shouldn't either. You have to do your research, boo. (My biggest pet peeve on *Top Model* is when a model wannabe can't name three models who aren't Victoria's Secret Angels and thinks high fashion is J.Crew.) You gotta ask questions, and you gotta observe everyone and everything you can. Do your homework, even if you gotta assign it yourself. Then leave your ill-prepared competition in the highlighter dust, because they can't keep up with your laser-focused Smize.

3

LIP GLOSS + PIZZA SAUCE = BOSS

· SOUTH AFRICA · 11/1/95 ·

"RUMP SHAKERS"

So many bootyful memories from my first *Sports Illustrated* cover.

👁 👁 *Tyra:* Have you ever been to a place where every which way you looked, there were miles and miles of sand so soft and fine that it got stuck in all the wrong places? It was 1996, and Argentinian model Valeria Mazza and I were in South Africa, prancing and dancing our way across this sand for the *Sports Illustrated* Swimsuit Issue. As I jumped up and down in my leopard-print bikini (roar!), I was worried about my gosh-darned cellulite. Yes, that's what was running through my head.

Now, models today are Photoshopped till they all have glass ass (so shiny you could check your lipstick in the reflection on their upper thighs), but twenty years ago, this wasn't the case, and when the issue dropped, I, with my stretch marks and the booty tooch, became the first black model to grace the cover. I shared it with cheetah-bikini-clad Argentinean blond Valeria, but I was still as happy as Vivian on that fire escape in *Pretty Woman*. (I love you, Julia!)

I musta been the only one who cared about my stretch marks. Flash forward a year.

I'm snoozin' away when my dreams are interrupted by a fire alarm. Actually, it's the phone. Ringing right next to my head. The day before, I'd had a shoot that required a nighttime setting, so I'd shot until the sun started to creep up over the New York City skyline. Now I had my eye mask on and the curtains drawn, determined to get some shut-eye.

My first *Sports Illustrated* cover with Valeria Mazza in the sands of South Africa.

But that phone.

I grabbed the receiver and got it somewhat close to my mouth without even opening my eyes.

"Smelllo?"

"Tyra, it's Elaine Farley. From *Sports Illustrated*."

Now I'm listening. I sit up and rip the mask off, my eyes wide-open. My stomach tenses—if she's calling me personally, instead of just sending a message through my agent, it must be something bad. I hope she's not calling to tell me they've axed me from the issue. Because the last time she called me, a few months ago, she informed me they were scrapping the entire shoot I did in Bodrum, Turkey. I was crushed. That shoot I did in that quaint ancient town surrounded by beautiful men with the sharpest bone structure and the most soulful eyes was so artistic. But the good news that came out of Elaine's mouth next was that they wanted to reshoot me on a beach. So I schlepped to the Bahamas to work with this new photographer named Russell James to re-shoot my spread.

Russell was cute as hell (retired male model—cheekbones, laser-blue eyes, long hair, Aussie accent, flip-flop-wearing 24-7—actually he was more like fine as hell), but that's all that was cute on that set 'cause his test pics we shot, Polaroids, looked to' up from the flo' up. Which means the final photos were gonna be wickitywack!

But I'm not bringing it up unless she does. I swallow.

"What's up?" I ask her, trying to sound as calm and not disappointed as I can.

"Tyra, you got the cover."

"Oh wow, coolio," I say. "With who?"

"No one."

"What? I'm by myself?"

"You're by yourself."

"No way!"

"Yes way!"

"No friggin' way!"

"Yes friggin' way!"

Not only was I going to be the first black model on the cover by herself, but this was also *Sports Illustrated*'s first dedicated swimsuit issue.

All of a sudden, I'm floating. It's so surreal, it's almost like I'm having an out-of-body experience. I'm looking at myself, sitting in bed, with the phone up to my ear and a look of utter disbelief on my face. Then, just as suddenly, I zoom back down into myself.

I thank Elaine. I hang up. I call Mama.

And that's when I start screaming.

Flash forward to the issue release party back in New York. I'm with my mama and daddy (ya know how I roll—party girl for life, right?), and we pull up to the party at the Industria studio—the coolest photo studio at the time—a place I'd been many times before for photo shoots.

But this is the first time they've had a three-story-high backlit photo of me in a red polka-dot bikini out front, glowing like the bat signal for all of lower Manhattan to see. I didn't walk into that party, I floated. I was Cinderella, Sleeping Beauty, and (caramel) Snow White all rolled into one. This was my mother-effing princess moment. I can say, without a hint of exaggeration, that it was one of the happiest days of my life (I remember I wore a Victoria's Secret camel-colored tube dress).

Every which way I turned, journalists were coming up to me, asking how it felt. "Amazing!" I'd say. "I can't believe this is happening; it's incredible."

Those answers were true.

But they weren't my whole story.

Then a reporter from BET came up to me. "So how does it feel to be the first black model on the cover of the *Sports Illustrated* Swimsuit Issue, Tyra?"

And that, that right there, was when I lost it. I started crying on their camera and couldn't stop (in fact, I'm crying right now, just thinking about it). I started telling them how I knew this moment was bigger than me, that I knew there were little black girls who were gonna see me on this cover and think that they were beautiful, too. They were gonna look at my photos and think, "That could be me someday."

This was history making. Yeah, it was a big moment for me and my career, but it was way bigger than that. It symbolized the beginning of a shift in thinking, where black models were standing front and center in a mass Americana way, after years of being crammed on the sexy-girl-next-door sidelines.

Makin' history in an itsy-bitsy teeny-weeny red polka-dot bikini as the first black model on the cover of the *Sports Illustrated* Swimsuit Issue.

Carolyn: When I was managing Tyra's career, I had agents tell me that I was the only parent they'd ever seen turn down opportunities for their child to make big money.

But Tyra's career was never just about money. It was also about breaking down barriers as a black model.

There were so many nos delivered, faxed, left on voice mail, FedExed, and snail-mailed through the USPS, and yes, those nos stung. But they were also a challenge—and about the only thing Tyra and I love more than ice cream is a challenge.

👁 👁 *Tyra:* As a kid, I went to the International Children's School (ICS) in Los Angeles, where the students were as L.A. as the Lakers but the teachers came from all over the world. My gymnastics teacher was Sri Lankan, my ballet teacher was French, my fourth-grade teacher was from Belize, and on and on. We were always learning about other cultures, and to this day, I still know how to do a Sri Lankan candle dance, without burning my arms, that I learned when I was in the third grade. Thanks, Ms. Gunasekera!

At ICS, most of the students were black, proud, and saying it loud. If you were a little black boy and could not recite Martin Luther King's "I Have a Dream" speech by heart, then forget you. It didn't matter how cute you were, how fast you could run, or how many Members Only jackets you had—you were a loser and weren't ever gonna amount to anything in life. At least, that's how it felt.

Every February, when Black History Month rolled around, we'd have a big assembly for the whole school and all the parents. In the fourth grade, I was out-of-my-mind excited to do my own speech, memorized by heart, about Vanessa Williams, the first black Miss America pageant winner. I was gonna talk about how much her win meant for the community and how talented I thought she was (I was gonna leave out the part about how everyone told me I looked like her, although that had me extra excited).

The day of the assembly, my best friend, Kenya Barris, and I are standing offstage, trying to one-up each other about who's gonna do better. I roll my eyes at Kenya. He's a boy, so he thinks he's gonna do better with his Dr. King speech, but I'm a girl, so I'm really gonna do better. We both know it.

The principal calls my name and I walk out there on that auditorium stage, and even though the lights are shining in my face,

I can still see Mama in the crowd, and she's smiling so big I can see her teeth all the way across the auditorium.

Carolyn: Tyra loooooooved her some Vanessa Williams. In fact, I love her, too. Years later, we'd watch that "The Right Stuff" video (the one with the fine-looking French man sippin' champagne in a bolo tie) over and over again, thinking "Nah nah nah nah, yeah yeah yeah. You go, V. Get it, girl."

Tyra wrote her Vanessa speech and would recite it to me over and over again. I'd help her with the inflections and give her advice about how to move around the stage and connect with the audience.

My clique of girlfriends came to the assembly with me, and I was braggin' it up as we sat down. "You don't know what you're about to hear and see, honey," I said. "TyTy is gonna blow everyone's minds!" I even leaned over to tell some strangers sitting in the row behind that my daughter was coming up next.

When Tyra came out onstage, she looked so cute in her little organza dress with a bow in her hair. As soon as she stepped up to the microphone, I sat up straight in my chair, just waiting. . . .

Tyra: I step up to the microphone. Visions of Vanessa's sash and tiara dance in my head. I part my lips. This boundary-busting black beauty queen fills my spirit.

I open my mouth wide.

And . . .

Carolyn: . . . nothing comes out.
Come on, baby. You got this.

Tyra: No, I don't.

I can't remember a single word of the speech I have been practicing in my mirror for the last six weeks. My mind is blank.

I am black.

I am proud.

I am riddled with stage fright.

Carolyn: She looks like a bullfrog. Her mouth is open and her tongue is coming out, but there are no words. Just bleh . . . bleh . . . bleh . . .

And the more she does that, the bigger her eyes get. Her shoulders start to hunch. She starts to look side to side.

Tyra: "Vanessss . . . aaaaaa . . . America . . . Missss . . ."

Tears start rolling down my cheeks as it dawns on me that this is really happening.

I can see Mama, who has the speech memorized herself from hearing me practice so damn much, and she's trying to mouth the words to me.

Carolyn: Oh, Lord. This is really happening.

Tyra: Kenya starts to snicker.

I can't take it anymore. I feel like Taylor Swift probably felt during the "Imma let you finish, but" moment: I want to be in a closet, under a rock, hiding in a Dumpster. Anywhere but up on the stage. So I run. I am a blur as I tear off that stage. The lunch lady is the first adult I see, and I run right into her arms. She gives me a big hug, and I'm boo-hooing into her shoulder. "It's all right, baby," she says, patting me on the back. "It's all right. There's always next year."

There's always next year?

Something about those words piss me off.

The tears dry up and my blood runs cold. I've worked so hard for this! My speech is really good! I'm not about to wait a whole 'nother gosh-darned year to do it!

Next year? Vanessa won *this* year!

I yank myself from the lunch lady's embrace, right when Kenya has finished his MLK speech, and head right back out on that stage, running just as fast as I can. I push Kenya out of the way, grab the mic like I'm Kanye about to drop the best verse of all time, and proceed to proclaim my love and adoration for Ms. Williams.

Carolyn: Wait a second.

Yes, she's back. But what's coming out of her mouth is not the speech she practiced ad nauseam. What she is saying is ad-libbed, off the cuff, improvised.

Raw.

Real.

It is better than she ever recited it; you can hear a pin drop in the auditorium. The whole crowd is in shock. She ran off that stage like a little lamb and came back out like a lioness. She grabbed that audience by the throat and didn't let 'em go, and when she's finished, I stand up screaming. "That's my baby! That's my daughter!"

Tyra: A standing ovation.

Wow.

I feel like someone just put a sash on my shoulder and a crown on my head. They're cheering my name. Mama is dabbing her eyes. Even Kenya is hooting and clapping.

That moment felt like royal magic. My experience at that assembly lodged something in my head. Being onstage? Making a statement? Not following lines? Oh yeah, I kinda liked it. I could get used to this entertaining people biz-ness. I was being celebrated for being authentic and for not giving up. And that felt damn good. But then . . .

A few summers later, something happened. And my body, well, it gave up on me.

In those three months, I grew three inches and lost thirty pounds, and I didn't look like anybody's beauty queen. I looked like a newborn giraffe still not sure what to do with its long-ass legs.

I'd grown so fast that my body couldn't catch up. My hips would pop in and out of their sockets as I walked. It hurt so badly I'd start to limp, trying to contort my limbs and walk in any weird way I could so as not to feel pain with every step. I had naturally dark circles under my eyes, but now they made me look like I had some type of illness, and I had these rabbit teeth that looked so big not even my forehead balanced them out.

Kenya was homies with this boy named Lorenzo, who I had a mad crush on. I was obsessed with him and would start blushing even when I spotted him all the way at the other end of the hall. Not only was Lorenzo as fine as a junior high boy could be, but his intense eyes pierced through my soul, even though we, ummm . . . never made eye contact. In my mind we were meant to be, and I badgered Kenya on the daily about Lorenzo. So finally, Kenya asked him.

"Yo, so what you think of Tyra?"

"Ugh, she's a skinny, ugly-ass monster."

Monster?

What?

I was crushed. Beyond heartbroken. I could deal with Lorenzo not wanting to be my boyfriend, but him thinking I was an ugly-ass monster? Get out the dustpan, 'cause that pounded me into powder on the floor.

Forget bein' onstage, playin' to the crowd, performing, or *anything* that involved other people.

The ugly-ass monster just wanted to hide.

The only good thing that came out of this time in my life was that I got all A's, because when the other kids would spill out after lunch to flirt and hang with their friends, I'd haul my still-hurtin' hips to the library and pretend that no one could see me if I just sat there with my face in a book.

My only C was in PE. Yeah, I was awkward and uncoordinated, but that subpar grade landed on my record because I didn't want to get undressed and expose my emaciated-looking body to my classmates (who barely knew my name) in the locker room. When I showed my report card to my dad, he skipped right past all those A's. His eyes narrowed and he handed it back to me. "What's up with that C?"

Well hell, there was no way I was gonna tell him that it was

The painful years, when my crush Lorenzo called me a "skinny, ugly-ass monster."

because I didn't want to get naked in front of girls who had started to grow breasts and hips when all I had was knees and elbows, so I just ran straight to my room and boo-hooed into my pillow.

Yeah, there was a whole lot of boo-hooing in those years.

Carolyn: Yeah, Tyra became skin and bones in one summer.

At first, I didn't think anything of it and figured her width would soon catch up with her height.

Except it didn't. I kept waiting, and so did she. While most of her friends were struggling to lose weight, Tyra was struggling to keep it on.

Our friends and family started to notice how skinny she was. "I don't know, Carolyn. Does she have an eating disorder?" they'd ask. "Is she anorexic?"

Every time we sat down to breakfast, lunch, dinner, she ate everything on her plate (and on her ice cream cone), but I still dragged her to doctor after doctor, trying to find out if there was anything medically or psychologically wrong.

Tyra: I was about the same height I am now but about sixty-five pounds lighter (that's, like, the size of a five-year-old child subtracted from my frame). Mama was so worried about me being too skinny (no thanks to my teachers, who kept calling her: "Carolyn, something is wrong with your girl.") that twice a week after school, I'd have to go to some doctor or another to get poked and prodded with needles. I felt like a science experiment, like something you'd see on a late-night TV movie called *Giraffe Girl*, where I'd stomp through the city and send everyone screaming and running away.

(What's crazy is that the same building that used to house the clinic where I'd have to go twice a week for tests is now part of an entertainment complex that is home to the *America's Next Top Model* headquarters. It took me a few weeks of walking through my office door to stop worrying that someone was going to come chasing after me with a needle.)

My brother and I were archrivals and he bullied the heck outta me at home (I still blame him for my elementary school mean streak—the whole I-must-be-a-bully-to-get-my-power-back thing), but for some reason, when it came to my weight, he rallied around me. It was like nobody was going to pick on his sister but him!

After school, I'd come home and he'd help me make shakes that we thought would help me gain weight. It wasn't anything as sophisticated as the protein powders of today, just whatever we could find in the kitchen that we thought might be fattening. Honey, sugar, bananas, peanut butter, cream cheese, Nestlé Quik, and ice cream would all go in the blender. Sometimes it was so sweet it felt like it might melt my teeth, but I'd suck it down like my life depended on it.

The shakes didn't work, but bless my brother: He tried.

Ma was my other biggest supporter, but she broke my heart one day when Kenya came to the door after school.

"Is Ty home?" he asked.

"I don't know," Mom said. "Let me see if her skinny butt is here!"

It was a throwaway comment that she probably hadn't thought twice about, but boy oh boy, it crushed my soul. She was my defender, my number one fan, and now she was making fun of me, too? I ran to my room and slammed the door so hard that they probably heard it in San Diego. That was when she realized just how much I was affected by my skeletal frame.

Carolyn: My previous job as a medical photographer had been at an orthopedic (muscles and bones) hospital, so I finally took Tyra to see one of the top doctors there to get a second opinion. The doctor ran some tests, and turns out, once again, they were negative. One doctor suggested she might have Marfan syndrome (what some people call giant's disease) because she had long arms and a long neck and had grown so quickly. But no.

"Do you have any photos of you and her father when you were her age?" he asked. I dug through our photo drawer and found pics of myself as a teenager when I was curvy enough that my mother made me wear a girdle and torpedo bra to keep everything from moving all around when I giggled. I then requested

My papa with his siblings. Need I indicate which one he is?
His daddy long-legs are screaming the answer!

some pics from her dad. The doctor looked at the photos and immediately shook his head. "There's nothing wrong with your daughter, Carolyn," he said. "Look at her dad in this photo. This severe thinness is just in her genes. I guarantee you that as soon as she hits puberty, everything else will catch up."

Giraffe Boy saved the day!

I was sitting on the sofa one day with my best friend, Jackie, a year or so later, when Tyra came home from school and walked through the living room into the kitchen.

Jackie raised her eyebrows. "What are those peaks on Tyra's chest?" she whispered.

"I don't know, Jackie," I whispered back. "They just appeared overnight."

Jackie craned her neck around the corner to see Tyra bending over, riffling through the fridge for some barbecue sauce. "Wow! And look at that growing booty!" We fell over ourselves laughing— quietly, of course, so Tyra couldn't hear us—and a little part of me relaxed inside. Everything the doctor had said would happen was happening. I didn't have to worry anymore, because Mother Nature had taken over! More important, Tyra didn't have to worry either.

👁 👁 *Tyra:* And then, something crazy happened. Something crazy on the first day of school in the ninth grade. By this time, I'd gained maybe ten pounds, so I was starting to fill in a little bit, but I was still brace-face from all the metal in my mouth and had the self-esteem of Sadness from Pixar's *Inside Out*.

I'm sitting on a bench, scuffing my shoes on the ground, and this girl appears in front of me. She's backlit and her crown of flaxen curls is glowing like a halo. Plus, she somehow looks good in her freakin' school uniform! Mine hangs like a laundry bag around my knees, but hers is short and cute and shows off her strong, long, toned legs.

And I think she's talking to me, but I can't understand a darned word that she is saying.

"Arumaah?"

Huh?

I do that movie thing where I check to see if there is anyone standing behind me, but there isn't; the bench is against a wall. She's clearly talking to me, and she's getting impatient that I'm not answering.

"Arumaaahda? Arumaaahda?"

Finally, it dawns on me that she and her laid-back California tongue are asking me, "Are you a model?"

I just snicker. A model? Puh-lease. . . . That's the most ridiculous thing I've ever heard. I'm an ugly-ass monster, not a model.

But it seemed like that girl, Miss Angel Locks, had a thing for monsters because she took me under her wing.

She'd turn the hallway into a runway and we'd practice perfecting our walks between the lockers. She took me to her favorite thrift store, where I bought a five-dollar dress that looked like couture—I wore it to the school Christmas dance when most everyone else was rocking Contempo Casuals and Jessica McClintock.

She even convinced me to forgo the hair-sprayed bangs, long-hair trend that everyone else was rocking and wear a pixie wig instead (and now, hardly a season goes by on *Top Model* when I'm not giving some girl a pixie cut. Oh, the tears!). I wasn't a professional model—posing for Polaroid cameras at lunchtime didn't count—but Angel Locks made me feel like I had an itty-bitty tad of potential.

When Angel Locks found out that Mama was a photographer (it didn't matter that she was a medical photographer who usually

In tenth grade, my friend convinced me to rock a pixie and wear this fly $5 vintage dress to the school Christmas dance.

shot anatomical dissections and deformities), she didn't miss a beat and asked my mom to take some pictures of her for her modeling portfolio.

Well, Mama didn't miss a beat either. . . .

Carolyn: I'd done some low-end lookbook fashion photography before, and hell, as much as I liked my day job, I didn't want to spend the rest of my life shooting infections and broken bones! Seeping wounds don't really have a good side, ya know?

This was one of my favorite cameras—it was large format, but I could handle it like a 35mm. It was heavy as hell, but I got some pretty nice biceps from lifting it. I loved that camera and all its heavy accessories, and kept it even after I retired!

So I figured this was win-win: Tyra's friend could get some photos for her portfolio, and I'd use 'em in mine, too. And Ty could tag along.

Tyra: One day after school, Angel Locks and I head to Ma's glamorous photo studio—the one in the hospital used to shoot detached limbs—so that she can take pictures of us in our eighth-grade graduation gowns, since they were the most glamorous dresses we owned. Oh, the ceremonial couture attire!

Mom starts with Angel Locks, and she's snapping away. They're working it like Mama's Annie Leibovitz and this shoot is going on the cover of *Vanity Fair.* "Beautiful! Gorgeous! Perfect! Yes, touch your hair like that, wonderful!"

Finally, Ma notices that I'm just standing there on the sidelines. "Come on, Tyra, let's get some pictures of you two together. Jump on in." I'm posing, Mom's snapping, but "gorgeous" is not what's coming out of her mouth. "Just relax a little, Ty," she says. "No, sweetie, relax. Now, put your chin down. Not that much . . . Up a little! Uh . . . not like that."

Ma is in her photo zone, in command of the set, making sure she's getting the shot. But I can't take it anymore. Finally, the misery dam breaks and all that frustration and pain (and jealousy) come flooding out. I run out of that medical studio crying down the hall, graduation dress flapping in my wake.

Carolyn: Yeah, I was in the zone. The wrong zone. I'd put my photographer hat on and tossed my mama one right out the window. Tyra was just standing there feeling like she'd just been awarded the Miss Awkward title and tripped on her way 'cross the stage to pick up her ill-fitting crown, and I didn't even notice. Every time I shouted praise for her friend, it was like shouting an insult at Tyra. And any constructive feedback on her posing probably felt like I was setting her up for a Comedy Central Roast. "Tyra Banks? Oh yeah, that fivehead be posing like a giraffe on Rollerblades. . . ."

👁 👁 *Tyra:* I lock myself in Mama's office and call my buddy Marisa. "My mom is horrible," I sob into the phone. "She's making me feel like crap. She's talking to Angel Locks like she's some goddess or something and I'm nothing. Like I'm not good enough. I can't stand it. I can't stand her!" (My mom, not Angel Locks, to be clear.)

👄 *Carolyn:* I could hear her yelling, "I hate her!" to God knows who, followed by screams that sounded like a velociraptor down the hall. Her friend was standing there looking confused and guilty. But I was the guilty one.

"Sorry, sweetie," I said, putting away my camera. "This shoot is over."

"I wonder if Häagen-Dazs is still open," I thought, "because I am going to have to figure out some way to make up for this."

👁 👁 *Tyra:* Angel Locks didn't know what the hell she was blabbering on about that first day of the ninth grade—I was not model material. This had proved it. You know that saying "a face only a mother could love"? Well, what the hell did it say about your face when your own mama couldn't capture a decent pic of it next to your stunning best friend?

👄 *Carolyn:* After that, Tyra really didn't want anybody taking her picture, not even if it was just a snapshot at a birthday party. A camera would come out and she'd just vanish, like she was a vampire and someone was about to open the black-out curtains. *Whoosh*, she was gone.

Then her braces came off, and she got used to having a few curves. Little by little, the gawk was replaced by grace.

I had started to get a little reputation with my fashion photography (that hospital studio started doubling as a fashion one more and more often), and I was doing shoots to help girls build up their portfolios. Sometimes Tyra would come with me as my assistant. I was makeup artist, hairdresser, photographer, film developer, and printmaker, and Tyra tagged along for the entire process, holding brushes and blow dryers, light meters and reflectors, and chilling with me in our laundry room that I'd transformed into a darkroom, complete with red lights and photo equipment balanced on top of the washer and dryer! When Tyra wasn't paying attention, the models on the shoots would whisper, "Your daughter needs to be in front of the camera, not holding blush brushes." You know, I looked at them like they were crazy. I knew Tyra had developed into a graceful, gazelle-like creature, but to me, she looked like a ballerina (must have been subliminal dancer dreams of mine), even though she'd begged me to pull her out of the one YMCA ballet class she took at age five.

Tyra: One day, I was walking through the Beverly Center mall (the same site of my infamous first kiss), when someone came running up to me and said he worked for Guess. "We think you should model, so call us," he said. In the late 1980s and early '90s, nothing was cooler than the Guess ads with bombshells like Claudia Schiffer and Stephanie Seymour, and this about blew my mind (though in retrospect, whoever claimed to be from Guess was probably lying, 'cause they weren't putting no black girls in Guess ads in 1989). I never called them because I imagined being taken advantage of by some crime spree model mafia, but it got me thinking. . . .

One of Mama's and my early shoots in our living room—I was fifteen, and this was clearly before I learned how to truly WERK it!

Carolyn: To my surprise, Tyra eventually decided she'd give the modeling thing a try. "If it works," she said, "maybe I can make a little extra money for college."

"Do it, baby," I said immediately. "Aren't you lucky that you'll have your very own private photographer and darkroom technician? Who just happens to be yo' mama! This is going to be fun!" Since I could shoot the photos, process the film, and develop the prints myself, we were rhet to go right away and didn't even have to worry about a budget!

When I was working as the director of the medical media department at the hospital and shooting fashion on the side.

Tyra: The first shoot we did was in the back of our apartment building. It wasn't really a yard, just a storage space for all the trash cans, with a humongous avocado tree that was always dropping fruit and making the sidewalks slick with green mush.

Mama did my makeup, a red lip with very little eyeshadow, and slicked my hair back into a bun (flauntin' that fivehead from day one!). I wore a black blazer and pear-shaped cubic zirconia earrings, and sat on a narrow set of red stairs that ran up to the apartment above us. The stairs were partially dry-rotted, full of splinters, and covered with peeling paint, and Mama had to move all over the place to make sure she didn't get any of the trash cans in the shot. Occasionally I'd have to swat a few avocado flies away. But the photos turned out good and went straight into my amateur portfolio. They were serene, regal, like a *Mona Lisa* for the *YM* generation.

Also, I was starting to forgive Mama for that disaster day in the medical office with Angel Locks. She gave me so many compliments along the way. "Oooh, baby girl, that is gorgeous. Turn right there. Perfect! We're getting that golden hour light!"

She did think I was beautiful.

Wow.

The first portfolio shot that Mama and I ever did— trash cans and rotting avocados just out of frame.

Carolyn: We went to a bridge downtown in East L.A. that was a favorite spot for photographers, because you got this light that looked like it was filtering down straight from heaven. Of course, to take advantage of that light, you had to dodge all the drug dealers and vagabonds who were shouting at you (it probably wasn't the best place for two women to be prancing around), but we did get some outstanding shots of Tyra on the railroad tracks. And to my surprise, my girl could move! Jumping, twisting, prancing, dancing. Click. Click. Click.

She was better than all the models I shot. I was confused by the quick turnaround. But I was one happy mama, cuz my baby looked so happy.

Tyra could move! I love these shots I took of her in downtown L.A., jumping and twisting all over the place.

Tyra: For that shoot, Mama put a fake braid on me, and a smoky eye. I wore a white peasant shirt, big hoop earrings, Levi's, and those cowboy shoe-boots. It was a '90s ensemble that would have made Lisa Bonet drool. (Yeah, Zoë, I was channeling your mama!)

We shot anywhere and everywhere, and Mama's inner Steven Meisel was flourishing. She was a connoisseur of light, even hauling my ass outta bed at the crack of dawn so that we could go to Souplantation (a buffet restaurant that sells—you guessed it!—lotsa soup) on Wilshire Boulevard before it opened to shoot at an exterior table with the dusty dawn streaming in lovely under the cantilevered roof, hitting me wearing a sailor shirt and a dusty vintage pillbox hat with faux crumpled flowers intertwining on the crown.

Carolyn: I always had my camera with me, so if we were driving and something caught my eye, we'd pull over and do an impromptu shoot. When we passed a courtyard with an electric blue door on Western Avenue, we just pulled up to the curb and hopped out to get some shots on the way home from the grocery store.

This was way before Instagram and fashion blogging, so people weren't used to seeing photo shoots on every corner. Traffic would slow, and people would crane their necks out their windows, trying to get a glimpse of the action and wondering what in the hell these two crazy ladies were up to.

Tyra: We lived on Hudson Avenue, a street that spanned multiple socioeconomic levels. Five blocks north of our

An example of the gorgeous light at Souplantation (with a prop muffin Mama brought from home).

Me looking sad because it's 5:45 a.m. and I'm realizing that modeling involves a lot of predawn call times.

Trying to keep my composure and not get distracted by the kids
playing right out of the frame.

apartment, it was mansions. Five blocks south, it was the hood, our part of Hudson. So Mama and my fifteen-year-old self headed north, to Hancock Park, and took pictures in the middle of the street while all the rich people probably sipped their morning coffee, peering out their windows wondering if they should enjoy the impromptu photo shoot view or call the cops.

Dodging traffic on the rich part
of Hudson Avenue.

Carolyn: We'd also stand on all kinds of sidewalks and wait for the traffic to pass, then scramble out to take some pictures and sprint back to the sidewalk before we got hit by a Mack truck or Mercedes. (Don't try this at home!) From looking at the photographs, though, you would never know it was guerrilla-style. Tyra looks poised and sophisticated, like she's the Queen of Beverly Hills (or the Fresh Princess of Bel-Air), when really, we were just right around the corner from the fake mastodons drowning in the gurgling, stinky La Brea Tar Pits.

A shoot we did at the La Brea Tar Pits— my hair wasn't cut like that; I just happened to swing my head at the moment Ma took the photo. And yeah, I styled myself. Don't hate.

👁️ 👁️ *Tyra:* The rich part of Hudson Avenue was two minutes and twenty worlds away from the ummm . . . not so rich part. As Mama and I played dodge 'em with the traffic, tryna get our shots before those crazy L.A. drivers flattened us like bubble gum, I had no idea that these photos were the very beginning of a career that would someday make it possible for me to live in the kind of houses we were shooting in front of: not a condo, apartment, or house, but a full-on *Dynasty*-style mansion.

Obviously, I forgave Mama for that disaster of a day in the medical photography studio. She hadn't meant any harm, and it was clear to me now that she more than believed in me. Mama was my number one supporter. We were ready to do this.

For real.

👄 *Carolyn:* Tyra had made a list of the top ten modeling agencies, so we started at the top.

Maybe the beret was a bit of foreshadowing, 'cause it wasn't too long after I took this pic that Tyra was heading to Paris.

Tyra: You'd walk into an agency, show your portfolio, then they'd look at it and tell you what was wrong with you. That was how I got introduced to some of the most broken feelings I've ever had in my entire life.

Carolyn: It took everything I had to keep myself from jumping over the counter and throttling these people. I was like, "What the hell are you talking about? Everywhere we go, people are telling her she should be a model, and then we get here and you tell her she doesn't have it? And needs to leave immediately?!"

I had to bite my tongue and keep my fightin' words to myself, because I could not believe the way these agents talked to Tyra and the other girls who came to see them. It was like they weren't even human.

Tyra would sit stone-faced listening to this cold, hard rejection, and I'd sit next to her, squeezing her hand or rubbing her back, doing anything I could to make it hurt less.

Tyra: Someone would take a look at my book for all of 2.5 seconds, then snap it shut and hand it back to me with a shake of the head.

"Well?" I'd ask.

"Your lips are too poochy."

"Huh? You won't sign me because my lips are too poochy?"

"And your feet are major flat."

"I need arches to model?"

"And your eyes are too far apart."

"What?"

"And don't even get me started on your calves."

"What about my calves?"

"They are clearly not in proportion to your thighs."

"So that's it?"

"Well, I could go on." She'd clear her throat. "If you want me to. . . ."

I did not. These were all kinds of crazy things that I had never even thought to be insecure about, and it left me in a daze, like I could barely follow what they were saying.

Others would put tight little smiles on their faces and say, "We already have a black girl." When they did that, it was almost like they expected me to nod and agree: "OMG, I am so sorry I even asked! Why, with two signed black girls, we'd revolt and take over the agency!"

Even the agency who represented Angel Locks turned me down. That hurt. Deep.

But I'd take it like an ice queen, then bawl my too-far-apart eyes out as soon as we got back to the car.

Carolyn: With my big, unfiltered mouth, as soon as we got back outside after those appointments, I'd let loose with the mother-effers this and the mother-effers that. "Don't you worry a bit, baby," I told Tyra. "They're the ones who are losing out." Though truth be told, after the fifth no, I wanted her to stop. "Screw this," I thought. "She's going to college and leaving this whole modeling mess behind."

👁 👁 *Tyra:* For a lot of girls, that first no is all it takes. They're done with modeling after that. And often, I don't blame them. More power to them, even, because they know themselves and know that this cutthroat business is not for them. 'Cause the rejection you're going to face as a working model is one hundred times worse than the rejection you will get just trying to get signed.

I always tell people, "Just 'cause you look like a model doesn't mean you gotta be one." You can't just have the look—you have to have the strength and fortitude to fight rejection every single day. That's why you hear so many sad stories about models' paths going scarily wrong.

But me . . . I was ready to fight.

"Come on, Mama," I said. "Let's just do one more."

So we walked into LA Models.

👄 *Carolyn:* First, they looked through every single photo in her portfolio. I kept expecting them to bring out a giant Sherlock Holmes magnifying glass for all the scrutinizing they were doing, so that they could get in there with a good look at her pupils.

Then they made her walk back and forth across the room. And do it again. And do it again. And again. It was like watching a tennis match, back and forth, back and forth, and I was getting dizzy just watching.

Finally, they told her she could stop pacing, but to just keep standing there. The agent we were meeting with started calling in other agents so that they could check Tyra out. They walked around her like she was cattle up for auction and they were tryna decide if they wanted to bid.

I was sitting on my hands and biting my tongue, getting more anxious by the minute. By now, I'd had enough of these people carving my daughter up, and this dissection had pushed me past my limit. I was just about to grab Tyra's hand and drag her out of there when they said, "OK, we'll sign you."

What?

I couldn't believe it.

"Just for runway work," they said. "Because you don't have the face for photos."

It was a stinging, backhanded compliment. What the hell were these fools talking about? She had a whole book of good photos! I'd been taking her picture all over town and she was getting better and better. I mean, she moved in front of the camera like a hip-hop ballerina star! I wasn't just saying that 'cause I was her mama, either (remember that first shoot with Angel Locks?).

So she'd gotten signed, and hell, I still wanted to clobber them.

👁 👁 *Tyra:* Mama was pissed, but I figured I had my (very flat) foot in the fashion door, and I'd just keep wiggling until it opened even more. LA Models was the only agency in town that was willing to give me a chance, and I still have a warm relationship today with Chrysta, the head of their runway division (I still look lovingly at the bus stop outside of their old office on Sunset Boulevard, next to the chili dog restaurant Carneys, every time I drive by). Shoot, I even started to do more than just fashion shows. A little catalog job here. A little second-rate magazine there. But eventually, it was time for me to move on, and it wasn't too long after I signed with a new agency (well it was probably about a year, but "wasn't too long" sounds so much better and more gangsta) that I and my not-fit-for-a-camera face got booked for a top magazine. *Seventeen* magazine, to be exact.

Even though I'd shot the photos, there was no guarantee that they'd make it into the magazine. Mama's and my rule was you have not booked the job until you are on the set, and you are not in the pictures until you see them printed and in your hands. Mama and I would be driving through the city when I'd spot a newsstand and make her cut across four lanes of traffic so that we could pull over on Robertson Boulevard, where I'd jump out and see if they had the new issue of *Seventeen*. Finally, one day, after a black BMW honked and gave Mama the finger as she swerved to get me to the curb, there it was. The new issue. I held my breath as I flipped through the pages, telling myself that I couldn't be too disappointed if it wasn't in there.

But there was sixteen-year-old me, staring back at sixteen-year-old glee! I did the running man right there on the sidewalk to celebrate. "You read it, you buy it!" the newsstand attendant yelled at me.

"Look!" I said, holding the spread up so he could see it. "It's me! In a magazine!"

"Two dollars!" he said. I bought four.

We headed straight to the new agency so I could show them. You could see my smile coming a mile away, and as soon as I walked in, the receptionist asked me why I was so happy.

"Look!" I said, spreading open the magazine on her desk and pointing at my pictures. "I'm in *Seventeen* magazine! Can you believe that? My first agency said I didn't have a face for camera."

That chick must have been sharpening her claws right before I walked in, because she just smiled a tense little smile, like she was about to let me in on a dark secret. "Black models don't have a chance in this industry," she said. "So I suggest you learn to type, because next year you'll be applying for my job."

I hope she had fun making her words into a salad and eating 'em for lunch every damn day at her desk, 'cause it wasn't too long after that when I went to Paris for my first season and booked twenty-five fashion shows. And two magazine covers. In three months.

Boom.

Carolyn: As excited as I was for Tyra that her teen modeling career had taken off, I had to admit there were parts of it that made me nervous. Some of those girls were just so gosh-darned skinny!

Tyra's own preteen and teenage years had been the Matterhorn of painful emotion because of her weight (more specifically, her lack thereof). She had been so unhappy in her skinny phase, and had struggled with so many self-esteem issues because of it. I'd seen her suffer, and I hated the thought that she might feel pressure to force herself back into that zone of battlin' her body instead of lovin' it. She was healthy and happy now, and I wanted her to stay that way.

But healthy and happy wasn't exactly the norm in the modeling world.

Backstage was always a flurry of nakedness, as girls would have just seconds to throw off one look and get into another, and what I saw back there frightened me: They were skeletons in silk slip dresses and winged eyeliner. I saw girls whose rib cages jutted out sharply enough that it looked like you might cut yourself if you went to give them a hug. When they'd bend over, their spines would look like some sort of medical photograph I'd taken, each vertebra so visible beneath their skin. And they weren't just skinny; they were hungry, too. I swear, if I had tossed a chicken wing into the middle of the room, some of them woulda ripped each other's wigs off to get at it. Not to eat it—no, no, no, too many calories—just to smell and maybe lick it to remind themselves what food tasted like.

The industry put a lot of pressure on these girls and never let them forget that the bigger they got, the smaller their paychecks got. They weren't starving themselves just to stay thin; they were trying to hold on to their livelihood. (Remember that before you choose to write a nasty comment on a superthin model's Instagram account. She's either naturally thin or trying to desperately hold on to her job.)

"The minute this biz doesn't feel good anymore, you get up and walk away," I told Tyra. "You can quit, and I will not be disappointed. You are not stuck here; you have a brain, and a brilliant, creative one at that. So the minute you feel like you have to suffer to keep your paycheck coming in, you have my blessing. You can leave. And you should leave."

👁 👁 *Tyra:* And she meant every word she said.

At the start of my modeling career, I could eat whatever I wanted. My food intake was crazy. I could eat a whole large pizza with two dozen buffalo wings if I wanted to (and often did), and if I ordered a burger, you had better bet I ordered it with cheese, extra bacon, with a side of onion rings dipped in ketchup and mayo, topped off with a superthick vanilla milkshake followed by a pint of coffee Häagen-Dazs for dessert. I was eating anything and everything. I had a fast metabolism and some serious youth on my side.

My Paris modeling agency had given me a planner to keep track of all my go-sees and appointments, so of course I used it to write down the addresses to all the design houses . . . and all the McDonald's and Häagen-Dazs locations in town. In between photo shoots or fashion shows, I'd chill for hours in those hard plastic ice-cream parlor seats, drinking coffee milkshakes because it tasted like home. It was my happy place among all those early-morning call times, French accents, and photo shoots that went late into the night.

I wasn't the only one, either—my #squad in Paris were models who hung out at McDonald's. Yeah, the cool clique. (Taylor Swift, you didn't know I had the first squad, huh? The Mickey D's Mannequins!) My best friend was a Canadian model named Jen who could match me calorie for calorie. We could have put a high school water polo or football team to shame with how we could throw down on some nuggets. And forget fancy food like foie gras and escargot—we were in France, child, so we wanted *French* fries! And lots of 'em.

But in addition to girls like me and Jen, who were food obsessed, not food repressed, there were plenty of models who had eating disorders. I remember one popular blond model who would brag to her boyfriend about how she'd eaten only an apple that day. While she seemed proud of her authoritarian calorie regime and talked about it as if it were a sign of her willpower and discipline, there were others who kept it well hidden. It had never occurred to me to throw up after a meal, so it took me a while to catch on to the fact that a lot of the I'm-so-stuffed-I'll-be-right-back girls weren't running to the bathroom 'cause they had tiny bladders.

It wasn't until later in my career that I realized how much these girls had suffered. My girls. My buddies in the biz. Ones I really cared about. They started to speak out about how they had struggled with eating disorders at the height of their careers. A throwaway comment from a well-meaning agent trying to protect his model's career—"You need to lose a few pounds before this season"—would prompt a crash diet that would spiral into a full-on medical and psychological disease. It was a prison, and they couldn't escape. No matter how beautiful, unique, or rich they were, they were still starving for success. Just writing this tugs at my heart. I wish I had known they were suffering back in the day. I would have tried to do something. What? I don't know. But something.

Anything.

Carolyn: At one fashion show, I chatted with a super-model who was six feet tall and thin as a wet string. She was slurping black coffee and sucking on a cigarette like it was her life source. After telling me she was hungry as she turned down the other half of my sandwich, she confessed to me that she lived on Marlboro Lights and caffeine to keep her weight down. "If I had one wish in the world," she said, exhaling a cloud of smoke like she was a Weber grill, "it would be to not be hungry anymore."

"What?" I was sure I hadn't heard her right. What about world peace, or curing cancer?

"I. Am. So. Hungry. All. The. Time," she repeated.

"Then why don't you eat?" I was two seconds away from stuffing my tuna sandwich into her purple-pouted mouth.

"Because I want to keep my job, Mom."

Yeah, she called me Mom. A lot of the girls did.

She might have been the one who didn't eat that day, but I was the one who felt faint. I had to go sit down. "I will never let that happen to my daughter," I thought. "I will drag Tyra out of here by her hair if she ever starts to think like that. And I won't go for the weave tracks. Oh, no. I'll grab deep down into those tracks to the cornrows near the scalp so she can't slip away."

Tyra: I lived in two body worlds at the beginning of my career. One was full of beautiful white girls who would be like, "OMG, you are so skinny I could die! I am so jealous!" The other was my beautiful African American community of friends and family, who were always trying to feed me macaroni and cheese and collard greens with extra ham hocks to fatten me up. "Fix TyTy a plate!" they'd yell when I walked in the door. "Shoot, fix her two plates! She needs to gain some weight!"

So when I did finally start to gain weight, I didn't really care. All the black people were clapping their hands and nodding their heads like my body was coming along nicely and I'd finally started listening to what they'd been telling me since I was twelve. I'd walk into the family barbecue on the Fourth of July and be hit with a chorus of "Ooh girl, turn around. You lookin' mighty fine now!"

The modeling world, on the other hand, felt differently. Like, 180 degrees differently.

They weren't happy.

In fact, they were pissed.

Carolyn: The first few pounds she gained weren't that big a deal. Tyra'd get up in the morning, tug a little harder to get her jeans on, then laugh about it before she sucked in, zipped 'em up, and went to work.

But the weight kept coming, and her curves filled out like a Renaissance muse.

Soon, the modeling agency started droppin' hints about her weight, and a hint from the agency isn't much of a hint. It's more like an order. "She needs to lose weight," they said.

She tried.

Sorta.

Maybe she'd have a salad for lunch, but then she'd get a piece of cheesecake to celebrate that she'd only had a salad. I thought she looked good. She thought she looked good. But you did not see curvy curves on the runway. At least not the kind Tyra started to grow.

Then her agent in the USA took us to lunch to tell us something. Tyra was excited because lunches with agents always consisted of good news. A major campaign booked. A product endorsement contract. Career-growing goodness.

👁 👁 *Tyra:* I will never forget that man and the look on his face. As I sat there trying to guess what huge job I'd booked, he had another conversation in mind. Basically, I was an old Toyota Corolla that had too many miles on it and was losing its resale value. "You've had your moment," he said, shaking his head. "There are only about two or three girls who can become icons every ten years, and you couldn't possibly do that. But guess what. You can be a catalog girl now."

The words fell out of his mouth so fast and so fluently that I knew this was a speech that he'd pulled out of his files for just such an occasion. This was the "You is over, bitch" lunch. I could tell he'd delivered it dozens of times before, to girls who'd had a successful season or two or three who no one wanted to book for big jobs anymore. I didn't dare say anything, but inside I thought, "That's not me." There was something deep down inside, some sorta spark, that knew I wasn't just one of those here today, gone tomorrow models. This wasn't about just a couple of years of modeling for me. I put college aside for this damn business. This modeling thing was something bigger. Not just a career, but a destiny.

My life's calling.

Right then and there, I knew there were bigger things ahead for me. Things that were bigger than even my own modeling career. I didn't know what they were, but I knew they were going to be major.

I sat there, silent, nodding like I understood and agreed with everything he said, but wishing that I had gone ahead and ordered cheesecake.

Not to eat it. To smash it in his damn face.

(Drake, you know what I mean, right, boo?)

Carolyn: After that man told Tyra not to let the door hit her big ol' butt on her way out, he had the nerve to offer me a job.

Tyra: Now I saw Mama scanning the table for something to smash in his face.

Apparently, since I was now an overweight outcast, they wanted her to take over and manage one of their supermodels. She was heroin-addicted and beyond a hot mess, but she was skinny and blond, so he said she still had a future.

Carolyn: No thank you, honey. No thank you.

I did not have the time, interest, or energy to mother some model who was throwing her potentially stratospheric future away by shooting it up her veins. I had my own baby to care for, who had just been disrespected big-time to her face. "You're a has-been, Tyra, but Mama, we've got someone else who you can get your hands on to make into a major star."

What the—?!

When Devin went off to college, I transformed his old room into
a command center for managing Tyra's career.

Even after all of this nonsense—yes, Tyra cried (and cried and cried)—we did not panic. She was still getting work. It wasn't as much work, but she was walkin' some runways and posin' in some magazines. She still had *somewhat* of a career.

Then when we were in Milan for fashion week, her Italian agency called me.

"Do you have pen?" the agent asked in his strong accent. "I want you write down what I saying."

I grabbed a nearby envelope and started jotting down every name that he listed, eight of the top fashion houses in Italy.

"What's this?" I asked.

"All designer no want to work with Tyra no more."

"OK. Why?

"*Perché* she too big," he said. "Mama, she need lose weight. Her career will be finish if she do not."

👁 👁 *Tyra:* Oh, Lordy . . . that Milan Fashion Week. I remember it like it was the day before yesterday. And he told her the list was growing. There were eight designers who didn't want to hire me this season. Last season, it had been four. I had been the It Girl, but now I was about to be the Out Girl, and I'd never rise anywhere near supermodel status. I bet you've been in a situation like this at some point in your life. Maybe you were the metaphorical It Girl at your job or in your relationship, then all of a sudden you ain't getting that promotion or the love of your life says they want to take a break. Now, no matter how solid you thought your self-esteem was, it's really looking more like Swiss cheese (one of those big, mouse-baiting cartoon chunks, all full of holes). We all know that we shouldn't care too much what other people think of us, and that we shouldn't rely on external validation, but damn. In these moments, that's hard. You'd have to be stone cold to weather these kinds of blows and not let them affect you. And you're getting to know me more and more with each page turn of this book, so as you now know—I was not stone cold.

Mama showed me the list in our tiny hotel room in Milan, as I was sitting on the bed. These were some of my favorite clients, people who had snapped me up when I first got to Europe, but now they were turning their noses up like I stank like French bleu cheese, and they didn't want anything to do with me. I knew that the list was only going to grow as my body grew.

I saw my whole career flash before my eyes. What the hell was I going to do now? I pictured myself selling Jacuzzis ("Just look at those jets. Have you ever seen such powerful jets on a tub?") or spritzing perfume on unsuspecting shoppers at the mall.

I burst into tears.

I wanted to keep modeling. I was kinda desperate. I'd lose weight. I'd try anything.

"Mommy, OK . . . um, OK," I cried. "I'm gonna skip meals,

and I won't eat that much. I can get a trainer, and I'll work out in the morning and at night. I'll count calories so I know exactly how much I'm taking in. Then I'll hit the sidewalk in Paris, NYC, and Milan and run five miles before bedtime every night."

Mama put her arms up to come in for a hug. Or so I thought. Instead, she grabbed my shoulders and shook me like salad dressing. "Stop it!" she shouted, her face so close to mine that I could feel her breath on my false eyelashes. "This is nothing to cry about, Miss Tyra I-worked-like-hell-to-get-here Banks."

"Huh?"

"You know what we're gonna do?"

"What?" I sniffled.

"We're gonna go eat pizza."

Then she ripped that list into confetti and threw it in the air.

Carolyn: Once that pizza was on the table, steaming hot with all those little pools of mozzarella cheese and shreds of fragrant fresh basil, that was when I started challenging Tyra.

What can you do if you want to stay in this industry?

Where do you see this kind of body, bodies like yours?

Instead of changing it, what can you do to use what you have?

If the straight line is no longer the option, what happens if you turn? Pivot. When you look to the right and the left, what do you see?

Now, let me tell you, I did not want Tyra to fall into the trap of thinking she had to live up to some silly idea of the "perfect" body. I'd seen that my whole life: women stretchin', sweatin', and starvin' themselves to get into a shape that their body ain't never supposed to be in in the first place.

Tyra was almost a supermodel, and if she was "too fat," what message did that send to the rest of us normal-ass women? Those of us who aren't six feet tall? Who have curves in all the "wrong" places? I was so damn sick of hearing that women's bodies should be this, that, or the other, but never loved and embraced for what they are. I want women to feel like their bodies and booties are beautiful. I couldn't preach it to the world, but I could start with my daughter.

Tyra: When she said "pizza," my first thought was "crazy." Then she started walking. Actually, it was more like marching. I followed like I was in bootcamp, and we found ourselves at our favorite pizzeria (it was actually a focacceria on Corso Magenta; I can almost taste that divine cheese now, as I write this). As soon as I smelled the smoke drifting out from that wood-fired oven, I started to calm down.

We sat at our usual table, in the corner by the window, where we could watch all the people coming in, the families and couples just getting off work. Mama took out a pen and handed it to me. As soon as we ordered, she gestured at the tabletop, which was covered in white butcher paper.

"Now," she said, "you are going to write down every client in this industry that likes ass."

"Ass?"

"Yes, that likes *your* ass."

"What do you mean?" I asked, still thinking she was crazy.

"Who likes ass?" she demanded.

"Um, Victoria's Secret?"

"Write it down!"

"*Sports Illustrated*?"

"Write it down!"

I was starting to catch on.

"Middle America!" I wrote it down.

"Who has an ass?" she asked.

"Cindy Crawford!"

"Write it down!"

"Claudia Schiffer!"

I wrote it down.

By the time we'd finished our pizza, I had a whole list of commercial clients who booked the bold and bootyful, and a list of models who had curves and were working and at the top of their game, past and present. I sat back and looked at the list, now mottled with grease stains and dots of tomato sauce, and I slowly started to smile.

My career didn't have to be over.

It just had to be different.

Mama had always called the fashion elite "those bosses in black," because while I worked with many wonderful, warm, and nurturing modeling agents, designers, magazine editors, and other powers that be (who I am still friends with today), there were just as many who lived up to the stereotypes: They never cracked a smile, gave out a hug, or wore anything that resembled a color. Those were the power people Mama didn't want getting to me.

Now Mama sat back and crossed her arms. She was smiling, too. "I will be damned if my baby starves for these BIBs."

I ripped the paper off that pizza table and took it back to our hotel.

Carolyn: I sent a fax to the agency, and they called me back almost as soon as it went through.

"Carolyn, what the heck is the list?"

"Those are her new clients."

"Tyra is a high-fashion model," they said. "She walks for Armani and Chanel. None of these clients you faxed are high fashion."

"Well, she ain't high fashion anymore," I said. "She ain't starvin'. She's changing."

"That is not the path for a black girl," they said. "It doesn't exist."

To be honest, that made me so mad I can't remember exactly what I said next.

But I'm sure it wasn't very nice.

👁 👁 *Tyra:* As angry as I was with the USA agent who had told me I was over, there was a grain of truth to it. True, it was my booty that got me booted from the world of high fashion earlier than I would have liked, but said booting was inevitable. I worked in a cold industry that was unapologetic in how it embraced the new and next and put the old out to pasture (in my case at the ripe old age of twenty-two).

At first, I was depressed to have to say sayonara to couture, but the more resistant the agency was, the more convinced I became that a girl-next-door path was my path, that modeling for the masses was what I was supposed to be doing. "You just need to lose some weight and you could be the next Iman. The next Linda," they pleaded. "You are not a curvy girl, really. Just lose the weight. And it's too soon for you to go commercial. You will never work in high fashion again."

"I don't want to be high fashion anymore," I said. "I'm bubbly, like Christie Brinkley. I don't drink, I don't smoke. I don't party and neither does Cindy Crawford. I'm not exotic, dammit—I'm the girl next door. I'm perfect for Victoria's Secret. Just like Stephanie Seymour."

Victoria's Secret wasn't going to book me, the agent said, because the girl next door was blond, baby, not black.

At that moment, I had flashbacks to that secretary, sad desk salad all stuck in her teeth, telling my brown skin it had better learn to type.

JUST CALL ME JOSEPHINE BANKS-ER

My introduction to Paris was, shall I say, shock and surprise. I was embraced in France as I never was in the United States. Paris didn't make me feel like I couldn't do something just because I was black. "Oui, oui, oui" is what I heard almost everywhere I went.

Paris was my Josephine Baker moment—I was getting booked for covers when no U.S. magazines would ever think of putting an unknown black model front and center. This is from a French *Elle* spread by photographer Gilles Bensimon that eventually became a cover for Spanish *Elle*.

But as soon as I landed in New York City, all I heard was "No, no, no." Just like the Destiny's Child song. (What up, Bey!) Every day of my career, I'd had someone telling me what black girls could and could not do. It was like they were reading it out of the Bible, 'cause they often said it like it was gospel.

"Black girls don't book for winter collection fashion shows, because they look better in summer swimsuits."

"Black girls aren't gonna get major advertising campaigns."

"Black girls don't book magazine covers."

"Black girls don't get cosmetic contracts."

I was so sick, so friggin' sick and tired, of always hearing about all the things that black girls couldn't do. I'd been on magazine covers, and I already had a contract with Cover Girl. I'd proved 'em wrong before. I could do it again.

"Get me a go-see with Victoria's Secret," I said to my agent.

BRAD, CHAD, AND TODD: I SEE YOU LOOKING!

I started to notice men checking me out right around the time I started to sprout boobs (I know—shocking, right?). But it was always the chocolate brothas who'd do the full-on stop-and-stare. Every once in a while, I'd catch a white guy looking out the corner of his eye, but if he ever knew that I knew he was lookin', he turned away super quick and pretended to be really into comparison shopping for the kitty litter, lawn chairs, or whatever else was in the aisle he just happened to be standing in at Target.

And not I-just-got-caught-checking-out-a-woman guilty, but I-just-got-caught-checking-out-a-black-woman guilty.

If the white guys in America had been conditioned not to think that black women were beautiful, the Europeans, child, they knew no such thing.

"Bonjour, mademoiselle, une belle fille! Très jolie!" I'd hear on the streets in France.

In Italy, Mama got it, too.

"Donna bella mamma!" they'd catcall.

"Why all these Italian men tryna talk to me?" she'd ask as she sipped her blood orange juice, sitting outside the *pensione* in Milan. "All 'bella donna' this and 'bella donna' that . . ."

It was not what we were used to back home.

Then, after Victoria's Secret and *Sports Illustrated*, that started to change. I had just as many white guys lining up at my signings, blonds and redheads coming up to tell me they had my poster in their dorm room or had saved all my magazine covers. White women would come up in the mall and ask if they could get a photo. "My sons are such fans! They just love you, Tyra!"

Huh? Your *American* sons?

It wasn't like I was itching to get hollered at (any female who has ever walked down the street in New York understands how annoying, and sometimes even frightening, that gets) or that I needed the validation. It's just that, after a while, I started to think that maybe something bigger was happening. Maybe the taboos about being attracted to other races were starting to be broken—men of all races could look at a black woman and, instead of immediately thinking, "Not my type" or "That *is* my type but not gonna share that desire with the world," think, "Yeah, I kinda like that."

Maybe there's a white/Asian/Latino/Native American man out there, right now, who met his wife when he saw a beautiful black girl across the bar at Chili's in the Dallas airport/on Match.com/sitting next to him in economics class and thought, "Whatever, Todd, just go for it. Ask her out. The worst thing she's gonna do is say no."

 Carolyn: And well, whaddaya know? Victoria's Secret up and booked my black baby girl.

Tyra: My first day on set, I was so excited! I kept telling myself, "You're at Victoria's Secret. The pizza butcher paper plan worked! You're at Victoria's Secret, TyTy!"

I got my makeup done and it looked OK. Decent.

Everyone was nice. They seemed excited I was there.

Everything was going really well.

Then I sat down for hair.

(If you know anything about African American hair, now is the time to hold your breath and pray for me. OK . . . inhale and hold!)

It took me about fifteen seconds to realize that this guy had *no* idea what to do with my hair. My black girl hair. He was clueless. Straight (pun intended) clueless. He'd brush a spot, stand back and look, then dart in and brush another spot. He was a mother bird building a nest with anything he could find lying around. A little bit of hair spray, a couple of squirts of mousse (yikes!), some water-based gel (double yikes!), brushing again, the curling iron, the flat iron, the blow dryer, the diffuser, water (triple yikes!) . . .

I knew I was in trouble when he doused my hairline with that water and brought out the curling iron to curl it up . . . wet!

I sat there with a smile plastered so hard on my face I felt like my cheeks were cracking. "It'll be OK," I told myself. "Trust him. He wouldn't be here if he didn't know what he was doing."

Except that he clearly didn't.

And I looked a hot mess.

Finally, I took a deep breath and made one last attempt to calm the panic that was seeping into my veins. "Maybe you're just being paranoid," I told myself. "And they *want* your hair to look like you just survived a tsunami. Yeah, maybe that's the look they're going for. This hairdo is kinda sexy, in a damsel-in-distress sorta way. . . ."

Except as soon as I stepped foot on set, I knew it wasn't just me who thought I looked cray-cray.

The photographer's reaction was written all over his face, and it just said, "Ew." The art director and stylist wouldn't make eye contact with me.

After just a few shots, I ummmmm . . . this is hard for me to write . . . I, uh . . . got sent home.

Modeling is all about rejection, and you learn to not take it too personally. But this, this was different. I felt utterly destroyed. My fabulously fantastic future had flashed before my eyes, and I liked what I'd seen.

Then just as quickly, it was yanked away. I felt like a bride left at the altar, standing there all done up in a white dress while her ex-groom-to-be zooms by with a wavy-haired, weaveless brunette on his arm and yells, "We goin' to Disneyland, bee-yotch!"

To say I was crushed is an understatement. I was eviscerated.

At this point in my career, I was a pro. I knew not to take every rejection personally, and I understood that not every model was going to be right for every client. There had to be some synergy there, where you get together and boom! Everything falls precisely into place—you're happy, the client's elated, and the pictures come out absolutely, positively friggin' fantastic. You couldn't expect that to happen every single time you stepped on set.

Except this wasn't just any set. This wasn't just any client.

This was Victoria's friggin' Secret.

My previous season for New York Fashion Week, I'd only booked five shows, and I used to do twenty-five! So as you can see, I had a helluva lot riding on this. My sent-home-self went home in a daze.

What about my destiny?

It was really over. Just like that?

Over the next year, I booked some jobs. People in the industry still knew who I was, and I still had a name. Sorta. No one was talking about what I had just done, was gonna do next, or how huge I was gonna be.

I'd go to Mama and cry and beg. "You have to do something,"

I'd plead with her. "Call the agency and tell them to call Victoria's Secret back. I need another chance."

Mama would listen and make all sorts of comforting murmurs, like "Uh-huh, baby. I know, I know."

"So you'll call them?" I'd ask, hopeful, as soon as she finished hearing me out.

"Hell, nah. You call them."

Carolyn: Now, I love my baby girl, and I will always have her back in whatever she does. But does that mean I'm gonna fight her battles for her? Like I told her that day:

Hell to the nah.

Tyra: The first hundred times we had that hell nah type of conversation, I thought Mama was just being scared—she was too much of a coward to call the agency and make my demands. Then it finally dawned on me one day: Carolyn London ain't never been no coward, and she wasn't being one now. She just literally wanted me to do it myself. Oh, Lord. Fight my own battles? There's no way I can do that. I need my mama.

And to my surprise, she was there for me. She dialed the agency's number (yay!) and then did the unthinkable. She threw the phone in my lap, ran out the room, and slammed the door.

What the—?

At the closing of that door, my agent answered the phone.

Dammit! I started to sweat; my shaky hands and I hung the phone up. In her face.

Now the phone was just staring at me. And I could feel my

This was our #BossBitch photo—foreheads on blast,
game faces on. Don't mess with us.

mom staring at me through the door. Mama wanted me to woman
up. She would never throw me under the bus, but until I got the
message, she'd throw me *out of* the bus, over and over again. I
just had to duck and roll and hope she threw me out near a
Häagen-Dazs.

So . . .

I picked up the phone.

"Um . . . you ummmm . . . you have to get me another sh-sh-shot
with ummmm . . . Vi-Vi-Victoria's Sssssecret," I stammered. "I

know I'm right for them. I just need another shot," I continued, my confidence growing with every word.

"Tyra, it's over with you and VS. They sent you home."

"It wasn't my fault. It. Wasn't. My. Fault," I said through tears.

"Fine, babe. I'll call them. Don't hold your breath."

She called me back in a week. Victoria's Secret had listened to whatever the heck she told them: I had one more chance.

Immediately, I busted into Eye of the Ty-ger mode. I was gonna train hard AF and knock 'em out. I knew what I needed to do, and it was all about my body. And I'm not talking about my abs, my arms and legs. I'm talking about the right kind of body that I needed on top of my head.

My hair.

The night before the comeback shoot, I had my trusty hairstylist, Oscar James, come to my apartment to do my do. He conditioned my hair, flat-ironed it, and styled it, then I wrapped it up as carefully as I could in a satin scarf, like my head was a fragile Fabergé egg. I barely slept, making sure every hour on the hour my scarf was still on my head. (Think Regina King in the opening scene of that flick we all love, *Friday*.)

The next morning, I walked on that Victoria's Secret set, whipped my scarf off, and was rhet to go. My hair was did, so I just waved a hello to the hairstylist on set (and stayed as far away from him as possible), and all I needed was makeup. I sat down in the chair, then as soon as the artist was finished, I excused myself (oh, that fake tummy ache worked like a charm) and scooted off to the bathroom, where I redid my entire face myself. I drew in my eyebrows closer together, dabbed just the right amount of shimmer on my cheeks, added more concealer to my natural raccoon-looking eyes, and sculpted my contour like my life depended on it.

My life didn't, but my career sure did.

I added a final dab of lip gloss to the center of my bottom lip and scooted back to the set. "Everything OK?" they asked.

"Yep," I said. "Everything is great."

"Your lips really pop beautifully under the lights," the stylist said.

I gave her a wink.

That gleam right there was my future, shining bright.

Carolyn: After that, Victoria's Secret didn't just book my black girl; they gave her a ten-year contract and put their first black girl on the cover of the catalog.

And that was just the *first* first. There were more to come.

+ First VS swimsuit edition cover girl
+ Original Angel
+ First black Angel
+ First black model with a VS contract
+ First black model to wear the VS Fantasy Bra
+ First black model to wear the Fantasy Bra . . . *again.*

Damn!

It wasn't too long after that when her *Sports Illustrated* Swimsuit Issue came whipping around the corner and damn near blew me away.

Those black model barriers that had always existed? Well, it was like they were made of baby back ribs and barbecue chicken, 'cause Tyra straight devoured 'em.

Tyra: Many years later, when *Sports Illustrated* celebrated fifty years of the Swimsuit Issue with a televised special on NBC, my itsy-bitsy teeny-weeny red polka-dot bikini from 1997 and I were honored with the title of third-best cover of all time. It was a fancy award show type of thing, televised for the world to see, and when they ranked me number three, I was supposed to walk on the stage and give a speech, like they do at the Oscars. Shoot, the ceremony *was* in the same theater where they shoot the Academy Awards, so I was nervous as I approached the stage. I didn't have anything planned and there was no speech tucked into my push-up bra, so I just got up there and said what came to mind and spoke from the heart, just like I'd done all those years before when I'd talked about Vanessa Williams and what it meant to me, as a young black girl, to see a black woman be crowned Miss America.

"A lot of the women here say it was their dream," I said. "But it wasn't my dream, because I didn't think it was possible. And I didn't think it was possible because of the color of my skin. . . . I want to thank *Sports Illustrated* . . . for thinking different, and I say 'different' without an *L-Y*, for being daring and for making every little black girl that year that saw that issue go, 'Oh my God, Mama, I think I'm pretty because a black girl's on the cover just like me.' I stand here representing everybody with a dream, to know that if you have a dream and you have tunnel vision, it can come true. But remember to dream bigger. Because if you do, those things can be reached, too."

I was so touched by the recognition, and the next day, I posted on social media about the experience and what I'd said.

The reactions I got were 180 degrees different.

Most black people were front and center, cheering me on. "Wow, girl, you did it!" "I remember where I was when I first saw that cover." "My son had it on his wall for ten years!"

Other races of the rainbow were clapping, too, but some were kinda rolling their eyes (you can always tell when an Instagram comment was written with an eye roll): "Why you gotta bring race into it? Nobody thinks like that anymore." And some even typed stuff like, "Get over it!"

At first, when I read those comments, it really upset me. There were serious issues and obstacles, challenges and struggles that I went through as a black model every single day of my career, and I wanted to acknowledge that. Not just for myself but also for all the other black models who had been made to feel less than, who'd been told over and over again that they weren't as beautiful and as valued; told countless times that a black model's place was in the back of the issue, but never front and center. I'd been through fashion hell and back (stuff I haven't even covered in this book—book two, maybe?) to get to where I was, and I wasn't the only one, and now some people were looking at me like I'd tripped in my heels and landed on the most coveted cover in the world?

Were they truly that blind?

Then I thought about it some more. Could there perhaps be a silver lining to this cloud of ignorance? (*Ignorant* does not mean stupid. It means lack of knowledge or awareness. Look it up.) A lot of the people making those comments were from a generation that had grown up seeing black models on Instagram looking like their lives and careers were easy, stress-free, and equal. Maybe they didn't see Jourdan Dunn, Joan Smalls, Chanel Iman, my *Top Model* girl Winnie Harlow, or the Jasmines—Jasmine Tookes and Jasmine "Golden Barbie" Sanders—and think, "There's a black model." Maybe they just saw those, and other successful beautiful black girls traveling the world, Smizing up the red carpet, and owning the runway and thought, "There's a model."

There's a positive and negative to this. Yes, we are moving in the right direction for many people to see past the skin color of a model they love, but we can't forget what it took to get here, or diminish the fact that black models still struggle a hell of a lot. You only have to read their long, heartfelt Instagram captions about dealing with incompetent hairdressers to get a sense of what they're dealing with. I'm so glad they now have a voice to speak up about these kinds of ongoing issues. Young people today might not think race in fashion is a big deal, but there are still plenty of bosses in black and board members in suits who do. And sadly, they're usually the ones in control of the covers, contracts, and campaigns and checks.

And straight up: I do not think I would have been able to make such a broad impact if I had stayed in high fashion. When I was first told to lose weight—a lot of weight—it felt like my world was ending. This was the first major pain point in my career (well not the *first* first; I'll save that living hell for another book), and thank God I had Mama there to help me pivot and go in a new direction. When one door of opportunity slams shut in your face, you don't turn around and go home, boo. Oh, no. You just go through that side door, and if that's closed, go through the back door, the cellar door, the attic—just get in the damn house!

Success is not a straight line. It's more like the PCH (that's the Pacific Coast Highway for you peeps who are not familiar with the Los Angeles coast): There are all sorts of curves and switchbacks and roadblocks and traffic jams and high cliffs and falling rocks, and you'll fall right into the Pacific Ocean if you're too busy staring at the scenery to drive. The important thing is to keep your eyes on the road and keep going. Stay focused. Don't stop. Don't turn back. And don't forget to enjoy the wild ride.

I believe in destiny, but too many people treat destiny like it's the po-po locking them up.

We all know those people who just give up as soon as something gets hard. "Well! I guess that wasn't in the stars/in the cards/meant to be/my path, so guess I'll just stop trying." They'd rather tell themselves that losing is their destiny and success is out of their control.

Wrong. (Where is that *America's Got Talent* red buzzer when I need it?)

I learned that from watching (drumroll, please!) my own mother-friggin' mama!

There were many ways in which my mother was a victim. She went through abusive relationships, she got taken advantage of, she got pregnant young, she was discriminated against, she was poor, she was black, she had no college degree, she was female. . . . The list goes on. But did she ever *think* of herself as a victim? Not for a damn second. If there was a Miss I Control My Destiny pageant, Carolyn London would have done a mind-blowing dance in the talent contest, had you ROTFLMAO with the I-can't-believe-she-just-said-that stuff she went ahead and said in the interview, and played the body accordion in the swimsuit competition. She would have won by miles and then never given up that crown. No matter what happened to her, she refused to accept it as her fate, and she refused to let it define who she was.

Carolyn: It's easy to say woe is me and go back to bed. It's comfortable and cozy in those flannel sheets where you get to just blame other people for everything that's gone wrong in your life. It is harder to get up and fight when life's drama stares you in the face. Did you hear what I said? Drama. Not trauma. Trauma is an uncontrollable circumstance that happens to you and requires therapy, counseling, and medical and/or psychological treatment.

Drama is an excuse.

Tyra: And me and Mama, we ain't the kinda girls who make excuses. So when destiny starts to push at you, that is your sign to push back at it. You push back, and you show that bitch who's bawse. Take off your earrings and get your girl to hold your purse if that's what you gotta do, 'cause you ain't going down without a fight.

And know that no matter what, you at least got two people in your corner backing you up: me and Mama. And we know when to come out swinging! If a door slams in your face, we'll tell you to look for the window. If the window's shut, well then, boo, you got elbows, don't you? Break that ish!

Climb, crawl, leapfrog, high-jump, pole-vault, catapult—do whatever you gotta do to get and stay where you need to be. And if you get a few scrapes and bruises along the way, cherish them. Those are your battle scars. They show that you put in some work, rolled with the punches, and learned a whole hell of a lot along the way.

Now, go get 'em, Tygers.

(Though, if there are any little girls or boys out there planning to do a speech on me, can I give you a word of advice? Write it down. That stuff is hard to remember. Actually, forget the script and speak from your fierce heart. And don't forget to Smize.)

4

AIN'T NO PARTY
LIKE A
PERIOD PARTY

Carolyn: I was so naive, so very naive, about the birds and the bees and . . . the blood. Even when I was pregnant with a baby growing in my belly, I still barely understood how that baby got there. My own mama never taught me about the facts of life (much less the rumors), so I was as in the dark as a vampire bat in a cave at midnight. It wasn't like things are now—where you can just Google any- and everything—so if you didn't get information from your parents, there weren't that many other legit places you were gonna get it. Sex education at school was clinical and brief, and crammed into one day where the girls and boys were split up.

Who knew what they taught the boys? For that matter, who knew what they taught the girls? I certainly didn't—I had the flu that day and missed it all. Every last bit of it.

I knew there was such a thing as a period, and that some of my friends had theirs already, but I had no idea what a period was. I didn't know what it looked like, what it felt like, or why it happened. So one day, when my stomach was hurting really bad and I found blood in my underwear, I immediately burst into tears. I thought I was dying and probably only had days to live.

My mom found me crouched on the stairwell and bawling. "Mommy, there's blood in my panties. I'm gonna *die!*"

"Oh, child please" she said. "That just means you're a woman now."

What?

"Let me get you some Kotex."

Ko-*who*?

Back in those days, pads were about the size of a diaper, and you wore them attached to a sort of belt that went around your waist and had these metal clampy things in the front and the back. Mommy showed me how to put it on, and then handed me a stack of pads. "Make sure you change it regularly," she said, "or you'll start to smell."

And that was the end of that lesson. I was a woman now, with no idea what the hell was going on. Was I gonna die soon? I still felt like I was. I didn't even know that having my period meant that now I could also have a baby.

I was left to fend for myself.

And I didn't fend very well.

When I got pregnant, my prior sexual experience consisted of some poking, prodding, pushing, and pain, but never any pleasure. I had met this older navy man who was cocky and intense and intimidated the hell outta me. He knew what he was doing, but me . . . I wasn't a virgin—I'd had sex once before and didn't know what was happening except for a lot of "ouch!"—but I was still as clueless as a kitten. This went here, that went there, he moved around and yep, we made a baby. At that time, being pregnant without a husband was an extremely shameful thing, and my parents were—you guessed it—extremely upset. At their urging, I called the one telephone number I had for Mr. Navy.

His mother answered the phone, and I told her the news.

"Honey," she said, "that's your problem." Then she hung up.

I was shocked, then numb, then crushed. Then feelings of worthlessness flooded in. Her abrupt dismissal of me and the baby growing inside me made me feel like I wasn't a person but merely a thing—actually, two worthless things—she needed to protect her son from.

I never wanted anything like that to happen to Tyra. Ever. So when her Aunt Flo came calling, I wasn't gonna just spill the beans. I was gonna add ketchup, mustard, brown sugar, molasses, onions, and bacon to those beans. (That analogy makes odd sense, but I thought I'd sneak in my recipe for doctoring up canned baked beans. They will make you wanna slap yo mama! But you better not.) What I'm trying to say is, I was gonna tell Tyra a helluva lot more than "You're a woman now."

Embarrassment and awkwardness—c'mon. Y'all two are invited to the lesson. Cuz Miss Tyra is going to know every damn bloody thing.

Tyra: All my friends were getting their periods. But me, I didn't get mine until I was fifteen; even in my "mature" state, though, it was still friggin' awful. I started to freak out as soon as I realized I was bleeding. Why? Because I was at my daddy's house and desperately did not want him to know.

I called Ma and told her that she needed to come get me—now!—and told her that under no circumstances was she to tell my dad why.

"Please, Ma, please. *Don't tell Daddy!*"

Carolyn: I told him. I didn't want to look like the crazy ex-wife, showing up to drag our daughter off with no explanation.

👁 👁 *Tyra:* Oh my God! She told him behind my back. I was devastated. "You're probably just spotting," he said on the phone to me an hour later. I wanted to die. *Die.* For one, *spotting*? How the hell did he even know what that was? And two, he wasn't supposed to know!

Damn you, Mama!

To this day, my dad still talks to me like I'm a little girl—"Buster, Daddy loves you," and he does it so singsongy, like he's some character on *Sesame Street*—so at the time, it mortified me to think I'd become a real woman under his roof when I knew he still felt and treated me like I still watched Big Bird. I'd even lied for four years and said I believed in Santa Claus after knowing it was my parents leaving Barbie camper vans and Holly Hobbie ovens under the Christmas tree. It wasn't that I wanted the extra presents. It was because I saw how much my dad enjoyed it, and I didn't want to take that joy away from him. (And the extra ColecoVision video game cartridges like *Frogger*, *Donkey Kong Jr.*, and *BurgerTime* from "Santa" didn't hurt.) So when I started my period, I think I freaked out because part of me wanted to stay a little girl—his little girl—forever.

Then, of course, Mama threw me this odd, strange, weird, wacky but kinda-beautiful-in-its-own-way celebration.

👄 *Carolyn:* I had always loved anthropology (the study of humans, not the store) and learning about different cultures and traditions all over the world. One day, I was watching a National Geographic special and saw that in almost every primitive culture, there was a rite of passage ceremony where the women would come together to honor a girl who had started her period and teach her all about it. It was a celebration of womanhood, and an acknowledgment of passing into another realm.

That got me thinking—what did we do for our women, American women? There was no ceremony, and there certainly was no celebration. All we got was a box of Kotex! That was when it hit me: I'd throw Tyra a period party.

And let me tell you, there ain't no period party like a Mama Carolyn period party. Right after I had the idea, I started planning, and when I told Tyra about it, she started giggling and couldn't stop. We invited all the teenage girls she was close to. I told them they didn't have to, but if they wanted, they could bring a gift. After all, this was a celebration, right?

Soon, I got a call from the mom of one of the girls. "What's this my daughter's talking about?" she asked. "She said she's going to a period party at Tyra's house?"

I explained the premise, and she laughed so hard she couldn't breathe. She said I was nuts. "You're invited, too," I told her.

"No, no, that's OK," she said. "You've got some wacky parenting techniques, but I trust you cuz Tyra is a good and healthy-minded girl. So you know what? You go right ahead. Is it a potluck? I can send over a dish."

Tyra: Why did I get my period so late? Because I was so thin. At least that's what my doctor said. Something about me not having enough body fat that stimulates the production of estrogen or something. Anyway, I'd already had my first kiss, which is probably a little backward for most girls. Still, the period party was very special, and from the time I first heard my mama's crazy idea, I couldn't stop laughing. None of my friends could believe Ma was doing this. Once again, they thought I had the craziest, coolest mom in the world.

Because I did.

Carolyn: Tyra's favorite color is yellow, so I decorated the house with yellow crepe paper garlands and balloons, and set out refreshments. I even had a cake made, with yellow frosting and flowers, and the exact words my mama had said to me when I got my period: "You're a Woman Now."

When I went to pick up the cake, the lady at the bakery asked what occasion the "Woman Now" cake was for. "It's for my daughter's period party," I said.

"Huh? What does that mean?"

I broke down the whole idea, and her jaw dropped.

"A what for what?" she asked, shocked. "Why would anyone want to celebrate something so horrible?"

Now I knew I was on the right track. I didn't want my daughter thinking that this thing that was happening to her, which was perfectly natural and happened to every woman, was horrible like this lady thought it was. So to rub it in the baker's face I said, "Hmmmm. Maybe I should have ordered red velvet with ruby-colored cream cheese frosting!"

The whole point of the period party was to illustrate that becoming a woman is wonderful, not shameful. The female reproductive system has given all of us life, but so many people scrunch their faces up and treat it like a horror curse. This isn't the prom scene in *Carrie*—there's nothing to be afraid of. The only pig in sight at the party was the bacon in my famous baked beans.

Tyra: I do think Ma was overcompensating a wee bit with the whole period party, but who the heck can blame her? Her own mother, my dear Grandmama, was so backward with the whole menstruation thing, my mama vowed that my experience would be the complete opposite. But I can't blame my granny for what she told my mama. I bet it was more than her mama told her. Also, seeing me freak out when I got mine at my dad's house, my mama saw firsthand that I already had so much shame connected to becoming a woman and said to herself, "I have to do *something* before my child goes crazy!"

I appreciate that she never wanted me to be ashamed of anything, or to think that there was something bad or dirty about my body. And to prove that, the period party had all kinds of bells and whistles and, of course, tons of TMI.

Carolyn: Most of the girls at Tyra's period party had started theirs, but I still gave them all the complete breakdown. I wanted them to understand everything, from what the blood means to why it happens once a month and where a tampon goes. I had charts of the female anatomy, and I pointed out every part by its actual name. We all had vulvas and labia, so why should we be too embarrassed to say the real words? Majoras, minoras, and clitorises, oh my!

The highlight of the party was when I brought out the menstruation gift basket, which was better than anything you could ever order from 1-800-Flowers. I had gone to the store and gotten one pack of practically everything: tampons with the applicator, tampons that you insert manually, panty liners, pads, feminine deodorant spray—even though I didn't use it, it was in the aisle, so I threw it in. I arranged it all with some bright yellow tissue paper and included some day-of-the-week panties, which completed the ultimate period goody bag.

I took the girls through each and every thing in that basket and explained what the items were for and how to use them. I opened up the boxes of tampons and pads so that the girls could touch them and see what they looked like outside the packaging.

I talked about how often you need to change tampons (to keep toxic shock away) and pads (to keep all kinda mess away), and talked about how they'd have to try out different types and brands to decide which was the most comfortable for them. When I was at the store, I'd specifically looked for the biggest Kotex I could find. "If you're worried about having accidents at night," I said as I held it up, "this will be your best friend, because it goes all the way up to your navel in the front, and all the way up your butt crack in the back." This was pre-"wings."

The girls' reactions to it all were pretty mixed. Confused. Excited. Downright disgusted.

"It's like a diaper!" they screamed while passing around the massive pad. "I couldn't even walk two feet in that!"

In between some of that disgust and embarrassment was a lot of excitement. Most of them had never talked about their periods so openly before, and in between the "yucks" and giggles, they asked questions about everything from whether using tampons takes away your virginity to wanting to know if other people can tell when you're on your period.

The highlight of the party, though, was when I brought out the ancient period belt I'd had to wear when I was a teenager. To their young eyes, I'm sure it looked like a torture device. I guess back in the day, it kind of was. Thank God (or whoever invented them) for pads with adhesive!

👁️ 👁️ *Tyra:* My friends did a love circle for me, where they all held hands and danced around me, and shouted out beautiful or funny stuff about me.

"You're so goofy and fun, Tyra."

"Bloody Tyra. Bloody Tyra," to the tune of Bloody Mary.

"Last to flow and bleed but first to help in our times of need."

My fave color, which was forced upon me by my paternal grandmom (long story) was on full blast on my cake, so it appeared it was made for Big Bird. We ate every drop of that sunshine bright cake, and I opened the gifts from my buddies, and Ma brought out a basket of "feminine products" that I was used to just passing by and ignoring in the supermarket aisle.

In addition to all the blood collectors, there were feminine douches and all this kind of stuff, and later my mom apologized big-time.

👄 *Carolyn:* The vagina is a self-cleaning oven. You don't need to flush anything up it unless your doctor says so. I learned that information after the party and regret telling Ty and her friends otherwise. Meanwhile, I caught her staring at the tampons like they were monsters.

👁️ 👁️ *Tyra:* Tampons are mysterious demons. At least that's what I thought touching one for the first time. How the heck was I supposed to get that rough thing up my you-know-what? Sorry, Ma. I know you want me to use the real V-word but "you-know-what" just seems a bit easier right now. Anyway, I vowed to never use them. Tampons, that is. Ever. But I'll never forget my future BFF—maxi pads. Yep, they were in there. Those pads were superthick, like an In-N-Out Double-Double hamburger. Mama was all excited, going on and on about the innovative, futuristic technology of the sticky stuff on the underside of the pads that miraculously adheres to one's underwear.

Carolyn: And then, we danced! All the girls formed a circle, and Tyra got in the middle and shook her booty (even though there wasn't much of it at the time) while we all clapped and sang around her. It was her moment, her day. She was a woman now, and she felt good about it. All the girls left wanting a period party, even if they'd already started, and I started throwing them for all my nieces. Before we even knew what popularity on the Internet was (heck, there was *no* Internet back then), my period parties went viral (within our ten-block radius).

Tyra: I stayed true to my word, and for about a year after I started my period, I said, "Oh, hell no!" to tampons. When I was on my period, my purse was like a diaper bag, half-full of cottony, superthick maxi pads. But one day, I was at school in class when I ran out of them.

Damn.

None of my friends used pads, so no one had any.

Damn again.

One girl slipped a tampon in my hand, and I immediately dropped it and was like—you guessed it—"Oh, *hell* no!"

In the bathroom, I decided to risk scent, dent, and accident (see below) and just balled up a bunch of toilet paper that resembled a baseball and stuck it in my underwear. Needless to say, it didn't work and started to slide around and break down into a mess. I went back to my friend and whispered, "OK, gimme that tampon. I'm going to do it."

She came with me to the bathroom and stood outside the stall, trying to coach me through it. "You got this, Ty." But, goodness gracious, I couldn't do it. The tampon just wouldn't budge. Not a bit. My friend then transformed from coach to cheerleader. "You can do it. I know you can. Relax and think that tampon's a man."

Her rhyming was ridiculous. Even more so because I was a virgin.

And to make matters worse, the clock was ticking. This bathroom stall period party was not taking place during lunch—we had snuck out of class, saying we both had to go to the bathroom, and I realized that even if we both had a case of violent food poisoning, we would still be taking too long. So, I finally gave up. More toilet paper was gonna have to do it for the rest of the day, this time folded in layers and not like something Derek Jeter or Jennie Finch would catch in their mitts. Fortunately, I still had my tampon bouquet from Mama, so once I got home, I could practice until I finally got the hang of it.

It took about five years.

And thank God—even it if had had real wings, there was no way a bulky pad would've flown on the Victoria's Secret runway.

SCENT, DENT, AND ACCIDENT:
THE THREE WAYS PEOPLE CAN TELL YOU'RE ON YOUR
PERIOD (AND THE THREE THINGS YOU WANT TO AVOID)

Scent:

Carolyn: When I was in junior high school, you could always tell some girls were on their periods because you could smell it. In some cultures, girls are not supposed to bathe when they are on their periods—and I respect that, but at the same time, it breaks my heart! It's hard to describe the smell of a period gone wrong, but you know it! Tyra has a term for it, but I don't want to say it. I'll let her crazy butt share it on TV someday. Knowing her, she probably already has. But in short, I told the girls at Tyra's period party that if they didn't want the world to know they were on their periods, they had to make sure to change their pads frequently and bathe every single darn day. Skipping showers while menstruating was out of the question. And I don't care how late you are to school or work. Get your booty in some water or else.

Dent:

Tyra: I'm sure I had this issue all the time with those ginormous pads back in the day. To me, the pads seemed as long and thick as the bread on a foot-long Subway sandwich. So I think you're kind of understanding what dent means now, right? It means that the pad is kind of sticking out and you can see it through your clothes. Especially when someone is wearing tight pants and the pad is just too long, it can look a hot mess. The situation is not as serious these days because some pads are as

134

thin as those micro-shaved slices of turkey they have at Subway. Don't know why I keep referring to Subway. They are not paying me. Not that they would pay me to compare their sandwiches to obsolete maxi pads.

Anyway, now I'm hungry.

Accident:

Carolyn: We all know what this one is—you bleed through your pad or tampon and it gets on your clothes. This is a junior high girl's worst nightmare, so I told the girls to change out whatever fluid catcher they were using before it filled up, and to always make sure they had plenty of pads and tampons on hand. Not every bathroom has vending machines (the lack of them should be a crime), and a lot of times when they do, they don't work, or the pads are as thick as (see Tyra's previous sandwich bread references). You should even have enough pads and tampons to share so that when that random, panicked woman on her first date with her future life partner comes running into the restroom exclaiming, "Does anyone have an extra tampon?!" you can save the day and maybe make a new friend. Even if you never see her again, you'll be her knight in shining tampon, and she'll tell the story at her anniversary parties forever.

IN ALL SERIOUSNESS:
WHY PERIOD PARTIES ARE SERIOUS BUSINESS

Tyra: I'm lucky to have my mom for so many reasons (I know this, and she knows this, and she knows I know this), and the period party was just one of them. When I was younger, I thought of ye olde PP as something silly that she'd done to keep me from being embarrassed about my body and to make me and my friends giggle. It wasn't until I got older that I fully realized the cultural significance of what she'd done. For so many women around the world, having a period is nothing to giggle about. They're not even embarrassed about it; they're downright shamed!

Thanks to my mom's gift basket, when I started my period, I had a whole smorgasbord of feminine products at my disposal, so if my virgin vagina and I opted for a pads-only lifestyle, that was on us. For many girls in developing countries, though, there's no choice about it. They'll use what's available—leaves, socks, et cetera—if anything's available at all. Many, especially displaced women living in refugee camps, don't even have access to private bathrooms where they can manage their periods in peace.

Just like my mom when she started, if girls don't have the right information about what is happening to them, they might not even know periods exist until they get theirs and—again, just like Mom—they find blood in their underwear and think they're dying or seriously ill.

Over the past few years, many activists and relief organizations have worked to bring some of these issues out of the girls' room (or lack thereof) and turned menstruation awareness into a global campaign (once again, my mama was ahead of her time). We can all start making things better for women around the world by breaking the taboo at home. Just talk about your period (or your daughter's/sister's/niece's/granddaughter's/et al.) like it's not a big, bad friggin' deal.

'Cause really, it's bloody not.

WAYS TO BREAK THE BLOODY TABOO

➤ **START EARLY:** If your daughter finds your pads or tampons and asks about them, don't start stuttering and say they're for getting the bathtub grout extra clean. Tell her for real what the heck they're for.

➤ **DON'T TREAT PERIODS AS A "GIRLS ONLY" ISSUE:** If your son finds your pads or tampons and asks about them, do the same damn thing and tell him what the heck they're for. "Well, Timmy . . ."

➤ **PUT TAMPONS ON THE GROCERY LIST:** Don't be embarrassed to ask your husband or boyfriend to buy your supplies. Households need toilet paper and dish soap. Households with women need pads and tampons (or menstrual cups if you're brave), and there's no shame in that game.

➤ **YOUR PERIOD IS NOT JUST "YOUR PROBLEM":** One, a period is natural and is not a problem, though it can cause problems. Two, if you're having sex with a man, then your period is something that affects both of you. If you're trying for a baby, he'll need to know about your period cycle; if you're not, he should be wrapping his friend up and also thanking the Crimson Wave gods every time your flow, well . . . flows!

➤ **THERE IS ONE MAJOR PERIOD TABOO:** Never, ever make fun of anyone who has an accident. There is definitely a special place in "hell no, now that was not nice and you know it" for people who see someone bleeding through her pants and decide to point, laugh, or not tell her she is a-leakin'.

5

8 WORDS TO WATCH OUT FOR

👁 👁 *Tyra:* Oh gosh, you haven't experienced a sex talk until you've had one from my mama. She is more raw than a dripping, bloody, grass-fed, ruby red rib eye in the kitchen at Outback Steakhouse. Body parts, body secretions, and body gyrations—she's gonna cover it all. She gave me the talk—the *real* talk—when I was thirteen, and at the time, I felt like she was being gross for grossness' sake. I gotta admit, though, the rawness worked: While many of my buddies were squirming in the sheets doing all kinds of uncensored lip-and-hip play with boys they weren't sure they even liked, I was only squirming in my seat from embarrassment at my mama's lack of lip censorship.

When I finally did decide to get down and dirty a few (*more* than a few!) years later, I remembered everything that my mama had said. Even if I didn't follow her advice 100 percent my first time, at least I knew what I was *supposed* to be doing (or more like *not* doing), and she was in my head the whole time.

Sounds weird, right? But it wasn't as creepy as it sounds. It was actually kind of ummmm . . . comforting.

👄 *Carolyn:* When Tyra turned eleven, we flew and buzzed through the birds-and-bees talk. That was easy. Simple. It wasn't much more than my baby girl had already heard from sex ed anyway, so it didn't take much longer than fifteen minutes. This goes there. That goes here. Then there's some action and all that makes a baby.

Easy. Done. Moving on.

As a mama, I was happy to check that box. I had done my duty.

Cut to the eve of Tyra's thirteenth birthday, and I start to think we might need to revisit this little biology lesson. We are fighting over the last slice of barbecue chicken pizza at California Pizza Kitchen. Tyra has an extra side of barbecue sauce she's dipping every bite in, and I have ranch dressing and am doing the same. One too many times, I overheard Tyra, her best bud Kenya, and her other friends talking quite colorfully about um . . . "relations." The sheer stupidity that these little girls and boys would spout about love, sex, and lovemaking was making me cringe. "You can tell if a guy has VD because he has a crazy look in his face."

What?

"I hear that if you stand on your head after sex, you won't get pregnant."

Oh, no.

"You can't get pregnant on your period anyway. That's impossible."

Oh, hell no.

You would have thought they were a bunch of sex-ed teachers and gynecologists from the way they were so sure of themselves, even though they were wrong about every damn thing. If my baby was hearing all of this nonsense and believing every bit of it, I knew I had to do an intervention stat.

But how?

Tyra: When I was in elementary school, Ma got me one of those *Where Did I Come From?* books. It was my favorite book, full of cartoons about what Mommy and Daddy had (yeah, down there) and what they did to make a baby. It was pretty edgy for its time. Shoot, most parents of today would blush about that darn book now, but Ma was always ten steps ahead. Then, when I got a little bit older, she got me one of those teenage body books that talk about everything from pubic hair sprouting to stinky armpits and crotch sweat. None of my friends had moms who even pretended to talk to them about sex, so whenever a group of them came over to my house, first thing they'd want to do was get out the body book. It'd be open on the floor, everyone poring over it like it was nothing they'd ever seen before (even though they had all the parts), and as soon as Ma would open the door or stick her head in, someone would squeal and throw the book under the bed.

Carolyn: "You don't have to do that," I'd always tell them. "I bought the damn thing. And I saw what page you're on. Interesting, ain't it?"

Tyra: She loved making them squirm.

Carolyn: Yep, I was real. Yeah, I was raw. I wanted to make sure my daughter didn't have to move forward blindly like I did. I wanted to have a talk with her, but her being a teenager, I knew she wouldn't want to have a talk with me.

I had to figure out how I could have this conversation without Tyra running away with a homework/friends-coming-over/time -to-go-to-bed/Mama-we-ate-all-the-barbecue-pizza-so-we-have-to -leave-now excuse. How could I get her in a place where she couldn't run and couldn't hide from all the rawness I was desperate to spout? I needed to take her as a hostage of sorts. A legal kidnapping of my own child. The "choo-choo" sound outside the restaurant window caught my ear and gave me my answer.

I'd put her on a train.

Tyra: Why the heck is my mom telling me we are going to take a train ride? She didn't even give me any notice. I want to spend my thirteenth birthday with my friends in L.A. at the Beverly Center mall window-shopping at Contempo Casuals and checking out boys who I know will never want my skinny butt (but heck, it doesn't hurt to look at them). But now I'm going to be on a darn choo-choo train with my mom to San Diego. Like I'm a child. Sexy.

What the heck is in San Diego anyway, besides the zoo? Does my mom really think I wanna look at monkeys, alligators, and preschoolers all day? I think San Diego is a port for the navy or something, so that means there are a lot of sailors out there and they wear those cute sailor suits. I'm gonna rock a white outfit head to toe so I can look like them. Yeah, I'm skinny and awkward, but they probably have been stuck on a submarine with no chicks for six months. Maybe they'll think I'm cute.

Carolyn: I'll never forget Tyra dressed in all white from head to toe. It was as if she had some sixth sense that her mama was gonna spill all the dirty, and she needed to be as saintly as possible to be able to survive the uninhibited truth attack that was approaching. Tyra was not thrilled with the idea of a train trip with her mama for her birthday. I knew she'd rather stay home and eat ice cream with her friends.

"San Diego? To the zoo? Ma, I'm about to be a teenager. You know the zoo is for babies." I wanted to tell her that this trip was to prep her for a different kind of wild animal: horny boys, the feral kind she was about to encounter in high school. And speaking of babies, the trip was also to protect her from birthing any too soon. But I held my tongue. I had to get her on that train and needed to make sure we were choo-choo-chooing away before I started my lesson. That way, she couldn't jump off.

Tyra: It is so obvious my mom wants to talk about sex. Like, duh. I don't know why she is hemming and hawing because usually she just starts spitting out all kinds of stuff other parents never would and with no shame whatsoever. Nervous she is not. Not ever.

I bet she wants to ask me if I've done it. Like, *it* it. I haven't even kissed yet, except my full-length mirror, which I French-kiss about once a week in preparation for the first time I kiss a boy. I gotta admit I look kinda sexy when I'm making out with my mirror. I keep my eyes slightly open so I can see myself, and I turn my head left and right like I see them do in the movies. I kinda make soft breathing noises, too. Nothing too freaky, just supersoft breaths to make it seem real. My mirror, on the other hand, looks like a teething baby got ahold of it and never let go, slobber running down the glass until it soaks my carpet.

Ma's still not broaching the real subject, so as the train rumbles down the tracks, I look out the window. We're sitting across from each other, and all of a sudden, she starts to snort. It's like this half laugh, half sneeze, like she knows something I don't and she's tryna keep it in. I start craning my neck. What is she laughing at?

Carolyn: The train is picking up speed, along with my pulse. How the hell am I gonna start this talk off? Where do I begin? It's like a freezing cold swimming pool, I guess—all you can do is hold your nose and jump right in. Still, I can't stop beating around the bush, making things uncomfortable by talking about how they're gonna get uncomfortable.

"Mama, I don't know what you're saying. You're not making any sense." She's right. I'm not making a damn bit of sense. I don't know where to begin. This kind of talk would have made my own mama jump off the Golden Gate Bridge into a pit of tarantulas on fire.

She rolls her eyes at me, then looks out the window. Right as we rumble by, some horses are going at it and having some very horsey sex. The whole train is watching, some passengers standing up and crossing to one side to catch a glimpse of the farm action.

Before I know it, I'm laughing at the irony and spraying ginger ale straight out my nose and all over Tyra. Her eyes go wide with disgust, probably half over the fact that her pristine white jeans are now covered with my soda snot, and half over the horsin' around that's taking place right outside my window.

I guess this is my cue, so I take a deep breath and start in. "So, Ty," I say, "we have talked about the birds and the bees—"

"Yeah, Ma. I read *Where Did I Come From?* a trillion times. This goes there. That goes here. Then there's some action and all that makes a baby. Blah, blah, blah."

Oh, she's an expert now, huh?

I shake my head slowly, because she doesn't know what she's in for.

"There is more to sex than here, there, and blah, blah, blah." I point out the window, referencing the horsin' around act the whole train just witnessed. "If that horse was a man and did what that male horse was doing to that female horse, he'd be up under the jail right now."

Now she's starting to squirm. Reality is setting in. "Ma, you're still talking crazy. . . ."

OK, that's it. Enough of me being vague. I decide to start in with the real stuff, and I used to be a medical photographer, so I can get *real* real. I start with feelings.

But not the kind you think.

👁 👁 *Tyra:* I sit there listening to her, and at first, I think she's "syndicating." This is what we call it in our family when Ma doesn't exactly know what she's talking about, but she's committed anyway. We started calling it this when I once asked her what it meant when a television show was syndicated.

"You know," she said. "It's popular . . . it's on reruns . . . a lot of people, y'know, watch it. . . ." I sat there listening, knowing she didn't fully know what she was talking about, but she was gonna keep on going until she ran out of words.

Carolyn: "I want to talk to you about feelings, Ty. How your body feels. A boy will touch you. Put his hands on you. And I have to say, it will feel good. Your body will respond in ways that you haven't felt before. You may even feel weak. Because as he touches you, caresses you, holds you, you feel like you are floating. He will say all kinds of things, and you will feel loved, as if he loved every ounce of your being. He will tell you he loves you. And those words will sound so good. And you will believe him. As your body continues to be caressed, and your bra is removed in a way you won't even remember it coming off, he will rub you in places never touched by anyone but your washcloth. As he kisses your neck, he will try to pull your underwear down. You will instinctively put your hand over his and tell him to stop. To leave your underwear alone and in place. He will comply and go back to doing whatever he did before he tried to remove your panties. Three minutes later, he will try again. And again, you will tell him to stop. So he stops. But kisses your neck again, squeezing you in all the places that he is learning second by second excite your body, which then turns on your waterworks, the secretions. And then . . . right at that moment . . . he will utter eight words that every young woman has to watch out for.

"Can
I
stick
it
in

a
little
bit?"

👁️ 👁️ *Tyra:* Now I know that my mom is officially crazy, and I will be forever scarred by those words she just said.

Can I stick it in a little bit?!

Really, Ma? *What the hell?*

My mom has truly just lost her mind.

And she's disgusting. What are you talking about "secretions"? Talking about vaginas getting wet (What? Yuck!) and how boys say certain things that will make your whole body go weak? Though I'm fake-smiling on the outside, my young brain is thinking she's gone buck-wild crazy and the inside of me is going, "No, no, no, that is not going to happen, this is not how this works, no one's gonna talk *me* into anything."

👄 *Carolyn:* As the train starts up again and picks up speed, I take a deep breath and inhale the courage of the Lion in *The Wiz*. "Ty," I say, "there is no such thing as 'a little bit.' 'Can I stick it in a little bit?" really means 'Can I stick it in a lotta bit?' A whole lotta bit. Like, the whole damn thing."

👁️ 👁️ *Tyra:* OK, I now vomit a little in the back of my throat. The train stops at the Carlsbad station, and a woman in a Hawaiian shirt grabs her luggage to get off. As she passes us, she smiles at my mom with that "You're doing the right thing, Mom" look. OK, hula shirt lady is crazy, too. Then right behind her, another woman, with purple espadrilles and lipstick that is bleeding so bad it's moments away from entering her nostrils, passes, but this time there's no knowing smile. She looks at my mom like she just spoon-fed me rat poison. I glare back at her with a Smize that can kill.

Only I can accuse my mama of insanity.

Carolyn: So how do I know those are the eight words my baby girl has got to watch out for?

From experience! From plain, cold (or hot) experience!

Tyra's daddy was my high school boyfriend and we did a lot of heavy petting and making out, but nothing really happened. To be honest, I never quite knew what he was doing and was too scared to ask. But again, nothing was going anywhere.

Then one day, something had indeed gone somewhere and it hurt. Also, I was shocked: I thought everything just bumped up against each other. I pushed him off me and ran straight to the bathroom, where I saw blood running down my leg.

Now, I did know enough to know that this meant I was no longer a virgin. The thought made me nauseated, and I sat right down on the toilet and cried. Needless to say, I never let him poke around down there again.

Tyra's daddy and I broke up, and he joined the air force. We slowly drifted apart when he was deployed to Vietnam, and I met a navy man (oh the irony of San Diego being a naval port!) who was much older than me. I was very intimidated by him. He told me, "I'm going to teach you how to be a real woman," as if being a real woman meant doing some stuff you didn't understand.

I didn't have anyone to tell me any better, so when he said I didn't have to worry about getting pregnant because he was just going to "put it in a little bit," I said OK.

"Put it in"? Shoot, I thought he meant "put it in motion."

But whoa, did I find out.

At first, I thought I had the stomach flu because I kept throwing

Tyra's daddy and me at my high school prom, shortly before he left for Vietnam.

up every morning. "Gosh," I thought. "This virus just won't go away."

Warning sign number one.

Then I thought my boobs were having a second growth spurt. All of a sudden, they got a lot bigger. Plus, they were so sore and tender.

Warning sign number two.

Maybe I was working out too much, getting too much exercise, because all I wanted to do was sleep all the time.

Warning sign number three.

All these dizzy spells are probably because I'm either sleeping too much or because I'm throwing up every morning.

Warning sign number four.

No period for three months.

Warning sign number . . . dang. Wham, bam, and not even a thank you, ma'am.

I'm pregnant.

I was not super slender but, at that time, I had a strong, athletic build with a six-pack belly that all my friends envied, so even by the time I was three months along and had figured out what was going on with me, I wasn't showing at all. It was like my tight abs were pushing the growing baby backward into my organs. After the manic sleepless nights, chronic nail biting, crying like an endless waterfall, thoughts of running away, thoughts of ending it all, I was shaking like a leaf, all day, every day. Finally, one late afternoon, I knew I couldn't wait any longer, and went into my parents' bedroom while my father was at work. I pressed my forehead against my mother's and whispered, "I'm gonna have a baby, Mama." She slowly backed off from me and under her breath, barely audible, she just kept saying no.

"No no no no no no no no no no no no no no no noooooo . . ."

My heart broke, because I had broken hers.

My Dubbie and my TyTy. I couldn't be prouder of both my children.

Tyra: My heart feels like it is ripping when I hear my mom talk about what she went through when she was seventeen. But that was the thing with her whole raw approach. She wasn't trying to shock me, or scare me, and she especially wasn't trying to shame me.

She was trying to save me.

She'd been through hell, and she was just trying to make sure that I didn't have to make that trip way down south, too.

Carolyn: My baby boy meant the world to me, and he has grown up to be one of the smartest people I've ever met in my life. He has three master's degrees and recently retired as a major after twenty-eight years in the United States Air Force. Overachiever? Um . . . yeah.

When he was nine years old, his favorite hobby was reading the *World Atlas*. Instead of playing video games, he could play the drums, guitar, and piano by ear, and he made the best zucchini bread I'd ever tasted!

I'm going to stop myself here, because I could brag up and down the block about my lil Dubbie (and I've been known to do it), who shares my ear-piercing laugh. From the moment he was born, my family overflowed with love for Devin, and I wouldn't trade him or the life we've had together for anything. But not all teen pregnancy stories have a happy ending, and I still think having a child at seventeen is way too early for the majority of people. Even if, like me, you always knew you wanted children.

Getting pregnant as a teenager was not something I wanted to happen to Tyra (I didn't want it to happen to any girl, for that matter, but you can't go about giving out sex talks to random teen girls on trains).

I didn't want her to get a disease, whether it could be cured with penicillin, staved off with a drug cocktail, or worse, result in death. I didn't want some man kissing her neck and lyin' to her and saying he loved her, when he really just wanted to feel her lovin'!

So yes, I told my daughter those eight words, and all other kinds of words, that men say to get inside a girl's head (and other body parts). "Now you're a step ahead," I told her when I finished. "You know what they're gonna say, so, years from now, when you do decide to have sex, you know what you're getting into. You're not naive, and you can give informed consent. You won't say yes to something you don't understand or were tricked into."

I made sure our time on that train wasn't all serious and that we had plenty of fun and that we laughed a lot. Because really, if you can't laugh about an awkward sex talk, what can you laugh about?

We ate ice cream. She put her feet up on the seat and I massaged her toes. We talked about the boys she thought were cute at the all-boys school. We kept talking and sharing all the way to San Diego, and the conversation didn't stop even when we got off the train. We kept yapping as we walked around and enjoyed the scenery in the Gaslamp Quarter. I didn't want her to look back on this conversation as a bad memory, so I was constantly giving some sweet sugar with the bitter medicine. It worked, because off the train, she had a chance to run away. But she didn't!

There were sailors everywhere, and Tyra kept saying she was just staring at their cool, white bell-bottom outfits. But you can't fool Mama.

Looks like my eight words came at the perfect time.

THE FIRST KISS

Tyra: My experiences of the sexual kind were nonexistent for about a year after the raw train talk. Then I touched a boy's privates—through pants!—before I even got my first kiss. It was at the Beverly Center mall, in the theater watching Matthew Broderick in *Biloxi Blues*. The owner of said nether region was Christian Bravo, who went to the all-boys school that was the counterpart to my all-girls school.

All the girls had crushes on Christian Bravo. He was fine as hell and had that I-care-but-I-don't-really-care swag that put the rest of the high school boys to shame. There was no way in hell he could ever like my skinny-minnie, awkward, and yet-to-master-the-Smize self. Mr. Bravo paid lil Miss Banks no mind. So when he started touching my leg when Matthew Broderick was at basic training, I was like, *"Huh?"* Soon, we were holding hands, and then—then!— he took my hand and went to put it on his knee. I moved at the same time, confusion ensued, and the next thing I knew, my hand

THINGS MEN WILL SAY
TO GET YOU TO HAVE SEX WITH THEM
—

(This isn't even everything!
Add more to our list at PerfectIsBoring.com.
Do it now—you'll be doing a public service.)

- Come on now, baby.
- You're being a baby.
- Are you afraid?
- Don't be a scaredy-cat.
- Can I just touch it?
- Will you just touch mine?
- I promise it won't hurt.
- I'll never hurt you.
- I just wanna feel you close.
- I know you want it as much as I do.
- Don't be a tease.
- Just hold it against you.
- If you loved me . . .
- Are you a woman or just a girl?
- If we do it, we'll be together forever.
- I don't wanna do it with anyone but you.
- Oh, so you're gonna leave me with blue balls?
- [Insert the name of whoever makes you feel insecure here] will do it if you won't.

And yes . . .
- Can I stick it in a little bit?

had landed right on his crotch. I yanked it back like I'd just been burned by a curling iron. And my face was definitely on fire. As soon as the credits started to roll, he leaned over and kissed me. Like I said, I'd practiced a ton with the mirror, but it never kissed back, so this was absolutely, positively . . .

. . . slobbery.

I didn't know what to do with my own tongue, much less another tongue in my mouth. It felt floppy, gooey, and slimy. I pulled back, and tried to play it cool. "You know, Chris," I said, "I really don't like kissing that way." As if I had tons of experience and knew what all the "other way" options were.

My first kiss, Christian Bravo. Every girl was obsessed with him, so I collaged his photo with a magazine cutout.

After the last credit rolled, I was up and out of my theater chair like I'd been shocked. As we walked past the food court and all the music stores selling tapes and this new thing called CDs, I walked fast and five mall stores ahead of him, all the way to the public RTD bus. I was way too embarrassed to even look at him again, and when the bus pulled up, I sprinted onto it and looked back just long enough to say bye. And from that moment on, I could never look him in the eye, so we never really talked again, but later that year, he started going out with this girl named Zara, who I had study hall with in the library. I was jealous of that lucky bee-yotch for years—because she probably knew how to kiss!

THE FIRST MAKE-OUT

Tyra: My first boyfriend was Byron Short. My oh my, he was an adorable green-eyed sweetheart, and a good soul. He was thirteen, I was thirteen. So, you get it—a whole lot of nothin' happened. Which is exactly what should be happening at thirteen! Then when I was fifteen, I fell in what I thought was love with this guy named Vé, who I met at a New Edition/ Bobby Brown/Al B. Sure concert at the Forum, where the L.A. Lakers played. Vé was eighteen, so not *that* much older, but old enough that the first time he came to my house, my stepdaddy took one look at him and said, "Your old ass needs to leave right now."

Of course, that only made me want Vé even more. I had some freedom—thanks to that RTD bus—so I'd traipse around town to meet him and hang out. Once, we even made out on the roof of a building at the La Brea Tar Pits. The tar pits kinda fart and also emit a smell, but I didn't care. I was in Vé's arms under the stars. Who cared if the air smelled like oil poop?

Vé and I also hung out at the mall. Every mall. A lot. He had a job at the Gap, but not in a mall. He worked at what I thought was a super classy Gap, in Westwood, near the campus of UCLA. So there I was, taking the bus to fancy Westwood to go see him fold T-shirts at work. I thought he was such a businessman because he had a j-o-b. And his folding game was on point.

After he'd get off work, we'd be on the phone all night listening to slow jams.

"Ty, who are you talking to?!"

"It's nobody, Mama, just Andria!" Then I'd go back to listening to Vé hum "Tenderoni" to me. So romantic, right? Well, it was to me.

I thought I was in love, and whenever my parents were gone, Vé would sneak over and we'd make out (fully clothed) in the living room after school. One day, we were going at it hot and heavy on the couch when he put his mouth to my ear, licked it, then whispered . . . those eight words.

O

M

G

I screamed, pushed him off me, and jumped up off the couch.

"She said you would say that!" I yelled. "She's not crazy! You said it just like she said you would!" Well, he didn't know what "she" I was talking about, but he did think I was crazy, and that I was trying to cry foul or something.

As I was hyperventilating from this surreal moment, my mind kept repeating, "Ma was right. Ma was right. *Ma was right!*" In fact, she was right about everything: I was feeling weak. He'd said sweet nothings in my ear. There were even secretions!

Needless to say, Vé and I did not have sex that day. Not even a little bit.

And we never did.

THE FIRST *IT* IT

Tyra: When I was about to graduate from high school, I had a boyfriend named Nicholas. He looked like a young Denzel Washington, and I'd met him in Westwood. In those days, all the girls would go to Westwood to just walk around the five-block radius in circles and try to meet dudes. It worked, and I ended up with a Denzel look-alike.

From the get-go, Mama didn't like his vibe. But I thought he was so suave. He'd come over after school when Ma was still at work, and we'd spend hours just lying on my bed in my room. Not even making out, just lying there for hours. And he'd stare into my eyes all intently and say sweet nothings to me. Not erotic or anything. Just deep. Experienced. I was intimidated and exhilarated at the same time.

I remember him touching my leg in a way that nobody had ever touched my leg before. "Hmm," I thought, "this is different." It was just an innocent touch but so different from Byron Short's thirteen-year-old touch, and even from Vé's. And whew, it felt nice. Really nice. Too nice. Tingly.

One night, we had gone to the movies and were making out afterward. After about thirty minutes of kisses that felt like heaven bathed in whipped cream (my fave dessert topping), he said those eight little words. But I didn't jump up. I didn't scream. I didn't yell, "She said you'd say that!" He didn't catch me off guard. I was prepared.

But really, I wasn't—sex was nothing like the movies. It was painful and awkward, and after, I cried!

I waited about three days, and then, yep, I knocked on you-know-who's door and said we needed to talk.

Carolyn: She said, "Mommy, I have to tell you something," and immediately started crying. I knew what was up. Immediately.

"Baby," I said, "what's wrong?" Even though I knew.

Through her blubbering, all the details came out. She stopped crying long enough to tell me that everything I'd told her would happen had happened. "Even though I did it," she said, "I didn't do it in a cloud. I did it because I wanted to."

I listened and comforted her the best I could. She said she had been mentally prepared so she didn't know why she was crying. I hugged her, dried her tears. Then I told her to get in the car now because the next stop was the drugstore to get some condoms.

Here's the thing: There are plenty of parents out there who think that abstinence education works for everyone, and that if you tell them not to have sex, they will listen and they won't do it. I wish that was always the case, and that everyone listened to the warnings and decided not to have sex until they were married! But if kids want to have sex, it's pretty difficult and at times impossible to stop them. You hear me? I wish we all could, though, believe me. Rarely can you stop them—but you can arm them! And I armed mine with a pack of Trojans, complete with nonoxynol-9.

HOW TO HANDLE BAD BOYFRIENDS

Carolyn: When it comes to the guy your daughter dates, you're not going to like all of them. In fact, you're probably not going to like most of them. The reason I didn't like the guy who took Tyra's virginity was because he'd come to my house with nothing to say. He'd never make eye contact, much less conversation. Sometimes he wouldn't even come in the house when he came to pick her up. Instead, he'd honk-honk and have my daughter running outside to jump in his car. That's a flag for me. You can't look me in the face, and can't have the most basic of conversations, then what the heck are you hiding?

Tyra: My brother goes on a first date on Halloween and then brings 'em home for Thanksgiving. He loves him some love. Me? I'll wait months, sometimes even more than a year, before I introduce someone I'm dating to the family. Cuz I know if I bring him around too soon, Ma won't be able to hide how she feels and I'll either immediately drop the dude or rebel against her and commit for way too long. Ma can sniff a hot mess, loser, or douche like a pig sniffs out truffles. And ugh—she's always right.

I dated one guy who was a Shakespearean actor, and I would try to coach him before he'd come over to the house. "Come on," I'd say. "You're an actor; you can do this. Just look my mom in the face. If you can't look her in the face, she's going to think you're shady."

Still, "Romeo" couldn't do it. Ma would walk in and he'd

suddenly start staring at the floor or get really interested in the remote control.

There were also other things wrong with him. Other "warning signs," should we say? He'd just had a big, successful movie come out, but he hadn't booked anything after that, and he wore one pair of beat-up shoes that looked about 101 years old. They were so broken down, the soles were coming loose and flapped as if they were having a conversation with the sidewalk. He also couldn't afford his own place and was late on the rent he owed the person he was crashing with.

Finally, Ma had had enough. "The man doesn't have a job, a car, a phone, shoes without holes, or eye contact, Tyra," she said. "What else do you need to see to know that you do not need to be with this fool?"

My hair-and-makeup team agreed. "Girl, it's the shoes," they said. "Even if you didn't know about the no ride and no phone, you should have taken one look at them broke-down shoes and gone runnin', boo."

When I finally did kick him to the curb, he filled up my answering machine with Shakespearean sonnets with stuff like, "Maiden Banks, thoust shall burn at thy stake for thy heart you hast brokest." I don't know about you but that don't sound like no Shakespeare I ever read.

Carolyn: I finally had to call and quote some Shakespear- ean N.W.A to "Romeo" and his crazy sonnet-ass attempts at threatening my baby. Dr. Dre, thanks for the words and "Beats" (see what I did there?) that sent that sorry fool running.

But that one time aside, I'm not really trying to jump into my kid's relationships. I probably knew that if I told Tyra, "You shouldn't be with him! You should leave him!" she would hold on tighter.

No matter who Tyra brought home, I think I was always polite and kept a pleasant smile on my face, even if I knew he was sweatin' because his butt knew I could see right through him, even if Tyra couldn't.

She had one boyfriend who was just talkin' about himself, talkin' about himself, talkin' about himself. All. The. Time. It was like there was no other conversation to be had in the room if it didn't pertain to him. I'm thinking, can my daughter not see what is going on here? It's all about him! He's not interested in what you are doing, where you're going, what you ate for breakfast. He made eggs and is stuck talking about how it was the best omelet ever created by humanity. It was just, argh! All through meals, he just would not stop. I'd leave the room, come back twenty minutes later, and he'd still be talking about himself.

One day, Tyra said to me, "You don't like him, do you, Mama?" I didn't lie, so I told her nope, I didn't, and gave her my reasons. "These are the traits I see," I said, "and this is my personal opinion. If you like him, then you go on and like him. And look on the bright side. He will never run out of things to say. About himself." I never tried to change her mind, but I could give her something to think about.

Tyra: Yep, I remember that dude. He loved him some him. Two weeks into our dating, we were at dinner one night and I said, "I could be anybody sitting here right now. You just need an audience." Ha ha ha. We laughed it off. I didn't pay too much attention to it. Cut to five years later and Mama finally yelled, "That mofo is so stuck on himself! And I'm sick of him! You're dating him, so you spend time with him. I'm done."

Soon after, when I was going through some very stressful times and would shake and cry in his arms and he still couldn't have a conversation that didn't focus on him, I was done, too.

Yep, she always knows.

BOYFRIEND RED FLAGS
AND HOW TO RECOGNIZE THEM

THE MAN: **THE HEARTBREAKER**

This was a musician who broke my baby's heart (and about ten other models' hearts). I damn near tied her ass down and said, "If you call him, I will disown you. Sit your butt right down here and let's start forgetting about him and his crazy-ass antics! I don't care how many Grammys he has!" (More on him if there's a book number 2.)

The flag: When you find out he's a serial heart crusher, don't give him the power to continue to break you. He dumps you? Don't chase him like all those other chicks did. Disappear, chile. David Copperfield his butt.

THE MAN: **THE MAMA'S BOY**

This pretty boy's mama wanted our children to be married after dating for only three weeks! She was obsessed with what their future children would look like. I really just tried to stay away from Tyra's time with Mr. Gorgeous as much as possible. Yeah, they looked cute together and he had a natural Smize, but that's about it.

The flag: A beautiful relationship is between two people, not three. Also, a pretty boy ain't worth his eyelashes if he doesn't also have a pretty personality to back up his angel baby face.

THE MAN: **THE UNSTABLE SCRUB**

Like Tyra said, this actor had no phone, no car, and no job, but plenty of time to leave threatening messages on her answering machine. He must have called from a pay phone.

The flag: The man who's always trying to bum a ride probably isn't going anywhere.

THE MAN: **THE GASLIGHTER**

This strong, strapping man cried to me like he was the victim, like all his wrongs (compulsive cheating and other unsavory shenanigans) were just because Tyra didn't see how much he loved her. I killed him with kindness until Ty was able to see that she wasn't crazy and put that nonstop soap opera in the past. He was young, restless, and not worth it. I knew I had to treat him nice. Had I told her he was dead wrong and she should run, she woulda held on.

The flag: No, you're not crazy. When you smell gasoline, there's a gaslighter in the midst.

THE MAN: **THE NARCISSIST**

This highly successful guy thought the world was a one-man act with an endless monologue about himself.

The flag: If you can't get a word in edgewise, he needs a mirror, not a girlfriend.

WE'RE ALL ROOTING
FOR YOU!

👁 👁 *Tyra:* What do you do when a girl comes up to you and asks you how to cover a black eye? Specifically, a black eye her boyfriend gave her?

Oh, and you've only got fifteen seconds to answer.

When I did my tour for *Tyra's Beauty Inside & Out*—a book that talked about all kinds of things, like dating, nutrition, and makeup (I even showed my face with and without makeup, way before #wokeuplikethis was the huge thing it is today)—I signed my books in Walmart as part of a Cover Girl promotion. (You could find me shopping up in Walmart, too; I bought a denim purse there that I carried until it was stained and falling apart. My model buddy Rebecca Romijn would always tease me about it: "Girl, I love you, but you're crazy and that purse is disgusting. It's got an ink blot on it!")

Girls (and the occasional guy) would stand in line for hours to get their books signed and ask me basic questions. Most were cheerful and bubbly—we'd rap for a few seconds about lip gloss and maybe snap a photo—but I'll never forget the girl who made everything come to a screeching halt (in my mind, at least). She couldn't have been more than sixteen or seventeen years old, with curly light brown hair and a smattering of cocoa sprinkles across her nose and cheeks. Her eyes were big and hazel, and one was puffy, bloodshot, swollen, and purpled with bruising.

I swear I hadn't heard her right.

"I'm sorry, sweetie," I said. "Could you repeat that?"

"Well, so, like, my boyfriend, he hit me," she said softly, shifting from foot to foot and twirling one of those curls through her fingers. "So now I have this black eye, and I need to find a good concealer so that I can cover it up when I go to school."

I had heard her right the first time, but I had no idea what to say. I'm sitting there, silent and dumbfounded, and my heart is breaking for this precious girl, and she's just smiling at me expectantly.

Security comes up. "Time's up, next!"

I should have jumped up and yelled to the whole crowd to wait while this girl and I went and found a private aisle and hashed out what was really going on right there, surrounded by laundry detergent and litter boxes and packs of tube socks. But instead, while I was in shock and couldn't think of what to say, she took her signed book back from me and disappeared into the crowd.

For the rest of the day, I kept signing like an autograph Roomba, but my mind didn't leave this girl. I was so down on myself. As someone in the public eye, I didn't want to just have fans. I wanted to connect with people and really make a difference in their lives. This girl had obviously come to me because she didn't know where else to go, and then she'd just slipped through my fingers.

I didn't want that to happen again, and I knew I had to do something where I could communicate with these girls in need for longer than the time it took to write L-o-v-e, T-y-r-a.

Carolyn: Sometimes Tyra would talk to a girl for five seconds, then worry about her for the next two days.

Girls would tell her all sorts of things—how their mother's boyfriend hit them in front of their mother, and Mama didn't do anything about it; how a boyfriend had forced her to give him oral sex while his friends were watching; or how they were afraid to eat lunch at school because the popular girls would walk by their table and call them fat if they saw them so much as take a bite out of an apple.

It was crazy. "Mama," Tyra would say, "these girls want to talk to me about extremely personal, deep stuff! It's like they don't have anyone else to talk to."

It would break her heart, and on many occasions her security team had to stop her from handing out her phone number and address.

But far and away, the number one thing she heard over and over again, from girls of all races, all socioeconomic levels, all body types, in different places all over the country was: I'm ugly. I'm ugly. I'm ugly.

They'd say things like "You're a model and I'll never be anything like you"; "I hate how I look and no one's ever gonna want me"; "My life is horrible and I know that if I was pretty, then everything would be better."

It tore her up. "Mama, these girls think I'm all that because they only see one side!" Tyra said to me one night after a signing. "They only see me after I've been in the glam chair for three hours being transformed. They don't see me popping pimples or getting my weave sewn in. They just see me smiling in interviews, unaware that just ten minutes before, you had to pull me outta the bathroom 'cause I was crying over some loser chump. They don't know that there's still a scared skinny-ass eleven-year-old inside me who was once called a monster."

So Tyra decided to swap photo ops for a mountaintop.

👁 👁 *Tyra:* I went to Girl Scout camp when I was a kid and loved it (to be fair, I didn't love it all, like how I'd hold my bowels for almost a week because I didn't want to go in those disgusting, fly-infested, rotten-smelling latrines). I was craving to connect with and inspire young girls wearing grubby clothes with rank armpits and twigs in their braids, where the only makeup is a layer of bug spray so thick you can scrape it off with your nails. And so I decided to found a camp of my own for girls.

Yep. Camp. Rough camp.

I decided to call it TZONE. I've never told this to anybody, but I thought of the name as a play on the *T* in my name (obvious) but also as the oily parts of your face (forehead, nose, chin) that are prone to breakouts. I wanted my TZONE girls to break out of their shells.

I believe self-esteem issues span all demos and all neighborhoods, and because I was funding the camp myself, I could choose the campers myself. I found girls from all over the place, from South Central to Beverly Hills, girls of all races and backgrounds, and girls who were straight-A students to ones who were barely staying out of trouble.

Later, when we started to get advisers, they put a stop to that. "Tyra, I'm sorry, but we're not paying for Becky with the good hair from Bel-Air to go to camp for free."

"But she has problems, too," I'd protest.

"Yeah, and her dad can afford a therapist."

That first year, my mama and I tried to do most of the prep ourselves. We rented this grubby white van and filled it up at the Price Club with everything we thought a camp full of girls might need (sanitary napkins, Band-Aids, extra flashlights). As soon as we got to camp, we didn't have anyplace to store all our supplies, so we smushed it all into our bunk and spent the rest of the week crawling over paper towels and toilet tissue rolls every time we went to get in bed.

Carolyn: The bunks we stayed in were full of critters running through the walls, but after the first few nights, we were so tired we became numb to them. "All right, rat-opossum-skunk, whatever you are," I'd think as I'd crawl onto my two-inch-thick mattress, "just shut up and go to sleep so we can sleep!"

TZONE was one of the most difficult projects I took on the whole time I worked with Tyra. Starting a nonprofit from scratch with no previous experience? Thank God I'm crazy, 'cause a saner mama woulda shook her head and walked right back out the room the minute she realized what she was in for. But I believed in TZONE just as much as Tyra did. From day one, I knew her career wasn't just about her, and we were putting that into practice. TZONE was as rewarding as it was hard, and the backstage drama of a fashion show ain't got nothing on a summer camp.

Tyra: Everybody was under strict order not to throw away any food in their bunks. All the girls listened. Some of the staff did not, and when a few of them snuck out of camp to go into town to McDonald's once, they tried to hide the evidence—a.k.a. the Big Mac wrappers—in their bunks.

Those fragrant wrappers might as well have been a neon sign for an all-night buffet. The staffers woke up to Yogi Bear trying to break down the door, and his roars echoed throughout camp, waking up everybody. The next morning, that staff's cabin was covered with claw marks.

Carolyn: That's true, camp food was nothing to write home about! Unless it was to say it was just plain ole nasty.

Tyra: During the day, typical camp activities made us hot, sweaty, and hungry, but nighttime was when the camp really came alive and became TZONE, where the breakouts would really happen. These were our night talks. We'd sit around the campfire or inside with candles and create a safe, no-judgments-not-even-an-eye-roll space to talk about the bigger, serious issues that girls face.

I'm obsessed with nicknames, and TyTy is mine. But at camp, my baby backs and Kansas City sauce–obsessed self was Barbeque or BBQ. And it was mandatory that every girl changed her name once she set foot on TZONE soil. Fun, new names made everyone feel safe. If I'm calling on a girl and asking her to talk about something really personal, like abuse, and I call her Kimena or Jasmine or Shelby, she might feel self-conscious and not share for fear of being judged.

But if I call her Rainbow or Panda or Smiles—or whatever she's nicknamed herself—she's reminded that she's in a safe place. I still think this is good advice for moms, parents, friends, teachers, everyone. Just like you know you're about to get a verbal whipping when ya mama calls you by your full name—"TYRA LYNNE BANKS, GET OVER HERE NOW!"—a nickname sends the opposite signal, like "Don't worry, boo, everything's gonna be all right. Let's talk."

My TZONE sisters. What's up, what's up, what's up!

Each night, I would focus on a different subject, like gender stereotypes, sex and relationships, or body image. What surprised me is that the body image night was the most emotional—and the feeling of "I'm ugly" got real specific.

We might as well have just passed out a multiple-choice quiz:

Q: Which body part do you hate the most?

    A. My boobs
    B. My butt
    C. My stomach
    D. My thighs
    E. The whole darn thing

Seven out of ten girls would have circled E.

Carolyn: Tyra came up with something she called the Mirror Exercise. I thought it was pretty clever.

Tyra: "Close your eyes," I'd say to the girls, "and imagine you're standing in front of a mirror, in the raw. There's no one else around, just you. You're in your bedroom, and you can really look at yourself."

I'd lead the discussion and call on girls to share. There were a lot of tears, as people talked about their eyes, their hips, their noses, their biracial features they disapproved of, and other things they wanted to change. But strangely, that was the easy part. I'd then ask them to pick something they liked. I went around the room, called on girls, and . . . crickets. Finally, with some prompting, a few girls started to speak up. They liked their smile, or their eyes, or their hair when they rock a high ponytail. It was contagious, and more and more girls started to speak up.

Just doing this started to heal so many of those negative thoughts they had, and you could feel the energy in the room lift as the girls jumped in to back each other up. I was giving myself major props.

Wow. My girls were feeling better about themselves already! Full steam ahead.

"Rainbow," I said, turning to the next girl, "do you want to share the one thing you found that you love about yourself?"

"No."

"Oh, you need more time? No prob, we can wait."

"No, I mean I don't have anything."

"You don't want to share?"

"If I had something to share, I would, but I can't find anything I love about myself."

I started to feel my heart sinking down into my trail-dirt-caked shoes. Even when I tried to prompt her by telling her what I saw—"I think you have the most wonderful smile, and I know women in Hollywood who would run someone over with a car to get cheekbones like yours"—she wouldn't take the bait. She hated herself from hair to toenails, and nothing the rest of us said could change her mind. I was crushed.

Rainbow was the first, but she wouldn't be the last. And get this. She was a counselor!

My jaw dropped when even more of our counselors—I'm talking women from twenty-one to forty years old—admitted that they also couldn't find anything about their bodies that they liked, much less loved.

That was when it really hit me: It's not just young girls who have serious self-esteem issues; it's women of all ages.

Every day in every way, from school hallways to fashion magazines, TV shows, and billboards, these girls and women were bombarded with the idea that females had to be perfect to even be counted. If you weren't skinny/stereotypically beautiful/rich/white with long hair/tiny waist/slim thighs et cetera, then you didn't matter. They felt like they'd never measure up, and they were crumbling under the pressure of perfection. My heart would ache for these girls who were so beat down by the world that they couldn't even muster a smidge of self-love.

As a model, I knew the publications and products other models and I were involved with contributed to girls not always feeling their best. I felt like it was my duty to be open about the smoke and mirrors that went into creating these images, and also give young women the tools to feel a lot better about themselves. I also wanted to remind them how unfair these pressures and expectations put upon them were. For instance, when you go to a concert and see Céline Dion on the stage belting away as her heart goes on and on, you don't go home feeling bad about your-self because you can't sing like her. When you see Steph Curry kill it on the court with a triple-double, you don't go home think-ing you suck at life because you can't sink that three. But when you see a woman in the media whose physicality is just as hard to obtain as a blindfolded half-court shot, society makes us feel like we're not good enough if *we* don't look like that, too. And that ain't fair.

It's hard out here for girls. And I think over the years, I have done a decent job uplifting a lot of women who just feel pushed down. And some of these out-of-the-box TyTy tactics were straight-up stolen. Yeah, I lifted some of them from my mama. And the learnings usually came when my signature Smize was on an ex-tended vacation. Whenever I was down on myself, she would ask me a ton of questions.

"So, he didn't call you back, huh?"

"Now, why does that bother you?"

"Did you really like him all that much?"

"Well, if you liked him that much, why didn't *you* call *him*?"

"Oh, you don't think you really liked him all that much? So hmmmm, perhaps this is an ego thing? What do you think?"

And on and on, until I'd looked at all sides of a situation and was feeling better. She didn't just up and solve my problems for me. She pretty much forced me to solve 'em myself.

Carolyn: Years later, when I saw Tyra up on that white couch for her talk show, talking to women about jealousy, high school popularity, the concept of "good" hair, or kissing her fat ass, I had to laugh.

It was a straight-up flashback to her night talks at TZONE. People always talked about how my baby girl seemed like a natural therapist—but honey, she learned it all from those camp crisis counselors.

TZONE planted the seeds for *The Tyra Banks Show* and her whole career, because this was where she began to see what her personal brand was all about: validating girls and teaching women to recognize their own beauty and self-worth. And to think all that can be traced back to cursing out cabin critters, rocking musty armpits, and dodging Yogi Bear!

I don't think I'd ever been so tired in all my life as I was after that first camp session. When Tyra and I were driving home, we pulled over at one of the first restaurants we saw, salivating at the sight of that red and yellow sign. It may have just been Golden Corral, but it was about ten steps up from the mystery meats and crazy casseroles we'd been chowing down on at camp for the past week.

After we went to town on that buffet spread, we sat in the van, rolled our windows down, and reclined our seats a little bit so we could talk while we digested our food. We both agreed that as exhausting as it was, and as hard as we'd worked, it had all been worth it.

Next thing I know, I'm blinking my eyes open and it's dark outside. I sit up in my seat—every store in that strip mall is closed and we're the only car in the massive parking lot. "Ty," I said, "what time is it?"

She groans. "I don't know, Mommy. I think it's . . . *ten o'clock?*"

We'd passed out right there and snoozed away for about six hours on the side of the highway! It's amazing we weren't robbed! Though I'm sure anyone would have taken one look at two dirty women snoring away in a van full of stuff and thought, "Nah, I ain't messin' with that trash!"

THE 3H TRIFECTA

Yeah, many of us know 5H stands for Fifth Harmony, even though they are just four now, but the 3H Trifecta is like a confidence rocket launcher that can send someone's I-am-in-love-with-me levels soaring into the Milky Way (the galaxy, not the candy bar, though that's good, too, if you're into chocolate. For the record, I am not. And don't get it twisted. I'm talking cocoa powder, not cocoa men).

FIRST: HUMOR: Jay Leno once told me that there's nothing you can't laugh at—eventually. But back during those night talks, I didn't even know I was doing that. I was just tryna get Caterpillar (or Daisy, or Pickles) to stop worrying about her buck teeth and have some fun! If you can make 'em laugh, you make 'em smile, and that's a step toward getting their minds off their drama, trauma, or psycho mama.

SECOND: "HEY, HOT HONEY!": Kick off internal self-esteem boosting with a lil external validation, even if someone is reluctant to accept it (sometimes it takes a while to sink). People with low self-esteem often don't trust themselves, so knowing that someone else thinks they're all that and a bag of salted caramel corn is like a jump start that can get the self-love buzzing.

THIRD: HARSH TRUTHS: This always comes last, after you've dissected the problem. "So yeah, one of your eyes is a little smaller than the other," I'd say to a girl after I'd just told her how stunning her eyes were and she pushed back. "So what you gonna do about it? Is that something you can change? No, right? Well, Imma show you what you can do about it, and child, it's called strategic eyeliner. Ever heard of that? No? Well you're about to become a master at it!"

Carolyn: Tyra can come up with some crazy mess. The 3H Trifecta? Lord. But she knows how to make something catchy so that people connect to it and repeat it over and over. I'm Smizing while booty tooching just writing this.

Tyra: Then *Coyote Ugly* called. The film was almost in the can, but they needed me back for one last scene with all the bartenders dancing together. I didn't understand why they needed my character back.

"I'm at my TZONE camp. I can't come. And anyways, my character, Zoe, went away to law school," I argued. "It doesn't make sense for her to be in that last bar scene prancing between whiskey bottles."

"Tyra, please," they begged. "Jerry really wants you in the scene!"

Finally, I agreed, but on one condition: I had to be able to leave straight from the TZONE grounds and be back before anybody even noticed I was gone. I'd made a commitment to these girls to be here the whole time, and I didn't want them to think I didn't take that commitment seriously. "OK," they said. "Helicopter coming your way."

It was a stealth mission. I took a bumpy-ass golf cart as far away from the campground as I could, then jumped in a helicopter and flew back to L.A. to film this final scene. For camp, I had really long cornrows, but in the film, my character, Zoe, wore a deep brown lace front wig. The hairstylist tried and tried, but no amount of cramming got my cornrows under that wig. "Ty, we're gonna have to cut 'em," she said. So we chop-chopped my braids, I danced on the bar one last time on camera, and then I choppered back to camp, all without the girls knowing I'd even been gone.

But the next morning in the dining hall, I'd barely dug into my bacon when I heard from across the room, "Hey BBQ, why'd you cut your hair?"

"Oh, ya know," I said, nervously sprinkling too much salt on my eggs, "change is good."

(*Side note: Jerry Bruckheimer talked me into being on the* Coyote Ugly *poster by promising me the lead in one of his movies. Seventeen years later, and I'm still waiting. Yo Jerry, what's up! I'm still waiting, and you never called! I thought Captain Tyra Sparrow had a pretty good ring to it, too. . . .*)

TZONE was just the beginning, and with everything I've done since, I've wanted to create spaces—mental, emotional, and physical—where women can boost their confidence and come together to support each other while having a heck of a lot of fun. When you start talking, heads start nodding, 'cause no matter what you are saying, someone in that room has been there before, and knows exactly what you're talking about.

THE WE'RE ALL ROOTING FOR YOU CHANT

That first summer of TZONE, I wrote a chant as Mama and I were pulling up to camp. I'd use it to greet the campers every time we all got together, and to this day, I'll occasionally be in a grocery store or at an airport, etc., and hear a voice start chanting:

My TZONE sister, what's up, what's up, what's up?

I got your back, girl; you know I'll back you up.

I'll be there for you, no ifs, no ands, no buts.

My TZONE sister, what's up, what's up, what's up?

This sentiment still holds true in every single thing I do. I got your back; I support you. No ifs, ands, or buts (but lots of butts. And period talk, too). You can substitute whatever you want for "TZONE sister." The only important thing is to chant it loud and chant it proud.

Carolyn: I had a dining room table in my life.

Sure, lotsa people have those, but mine was darn special. The people in the chairs, that is. Friends, cousins, aunts, neighbors, sisters—a support group where we cried occasionally but spent most of our time laughing our asses off.

We'd talk family, men, relationships, work, our children.

TZONE was one of the most difficult projects I ever did with Tyra. But it was all worth it—even the bear scare!

Often, our kids were there, too, playing off to the side, putting together a dance routine or drawing with crayons. They heard everything, because the dining room table was out in the open, and we had nothing to hide. These were women who didn't necessarily have men in their lives, but they took damn good care of their children, and we took damn good care of each other.

I could not have done a lot of things that I was able to accomplish in my life if I had not had the support that came from being surrounded by these women.

Tyra grew up seeing that, and her whole career has been

her way of taking that dining room table and adding a whole lot of extra chairs. Starting all the way back with that autograph table at Walmart. Like one of those Outstanding in the Field dinners she's so obsessed with (Google it; you'll see what I mean), she's tryna build the biggest table the world has ever seen. Usually only females are invited, but woke men . . . there are an unlimited number of seats for you to sit your butt down with her, too.

👁 👁 *Tyra:* Whenever I hear a woman say, "I don't trust girls; I can't stand girls," I just think, "Girl, is it 'cause you shady?" What kind of women are you attracting that you can't trust? And don't even give me that "I'm just so pretty that they're all jealous" BS. That just makes me roll my eyes so hard they might fall right out my head.

I've been a supermodel and I have been surrounded by wonderful, super close female friends my entire life. In the modeling world, I always looked up to Cindy Crawford because she was a girls' girl just like me. Even throughout her career, she had all these guys salivating after her, but she still got major cosmetics contracts because she appealed to women as well.

I recently had dinner with her at Shutters in Santa Monica, and I could see the whole restaurant freaking out and craning their necks because there were two supermodels having dinner, just one-on-one. I have to admit—I was kinda freaking out, too, because she's been my idol for decades and she's still warm and supportive and giving me advice.

Contrast this with another girl date I went on with Ms. WhoShallRemainNameless, but let's just say she was the wife of a well-known person. People had always told us that we would get along, so we finally met for dinner at a restaurant in Beverly Hills.

From the minute we sat down, we were hootin' and carrying on and hitting each other on the shoulder 'cause we were laughing so hard. I walked out of that restaurant thinking, "I just met my new best friend."

So I was texting her.

And calling her.

And texting. And calling, tryna set up our next hang, and getting nothing. Finally, I called our mutual friend.

"Oh my God," I said. "She disappeared. Is she OK?"

My friend hemmed and hawed for a minute and told me the woman was fine. "It's just that, after you guys had dinner, she said, 'There is not that much coolness and niceness in the world. I don't trust nice girls like Tyra. At least with a bitch, I can see what's coming.'"

Now, who knows if she'd just been wronged by wolves in sheep's stilettos too many times, but when I heard that, I was pretty hurt. I was always taught to put the sisters ahead of the misters, so bumping into a sister who didn't share this POV was always painful.

So what do I ask women who say they don't trust other females?

"You ever been hurt by a guy?"

"Yeah, girl, my last two boyfriends cheated on me."

"And you have a new man now?"

"Yeah, he's my soul mate! I'm soooo in love with him!"

"So you can trust men again and again and again! Why can't you do the same for girls?"

'Cause we're all rooting for you.

BITCHES AND BULLIES

👁 👁 *Tyra:* I was the leader of the pack and the queen of the four-square court, and I wanted everyone to bow down.

This was fifth grade, and my clique of bossy, bratty girls ruled the playground like the cornrowed, pigtailed mafia. Every week, we'd kick someone out of our clique if they got on someone's (usually my) bad side; they'd spend recesses all by their lonesome, swinging on the swings and draggin' their feet in the sandbox.

One week, the clique even rose up against me and kicked me out of the group.

What?

You'd think I woulda learned a lesson then, but as soon as they let me back in, I picked up right where I'd left off: being the queen of mean and tellin' everybody what the heck to do.

Simone Green (name has been changed for the about-to-be-obvious reasons) was the leader of our rival clique (ooh, so cutthroat!), was just as much of a bitch in training as I was, and had about twenty pounds on my butt. So, when she wanted to play four square one afternoon, I seized the opportunity to shut her down and assert my dominance.

"I wanna play," she said.

"No," I snapped back. "The game is l-o-c-k locked." In kid world, l-o-c-k locked was an unbreakable law. It instilled the fear of God in the elementary school set. To challenge it was to go against the rules of nature.

But I guess the rules of nature hadn't met Simone.

"Lemme play," she said again, trying to swipe that red rubber ball out of my ashy hands.

189

I wrapped my arms around the ball like it was made of rubies and held tight. "No. The. Game. Is. L-o-c-k locked. To. Fat. People."

So she swung on me.

She wanted to kick my ass, and I deserved it. We fought, right there in the middle of the four-square court—pulling hair, ripping at uniform shirts, slapping, swinging, screeching, clawing, kicking. . . . One of our teachers was Bill Cosby's brother, and he stood by, watching the whole thing.

"Mr. Cosby! Mr. Cosby! You gonna break it up?" some kids yelled at him.

"Nah," he said. "Let those two bullies fight."

He knew we both needed some sense knocked into our heads. Finally, another teacher came along, broke it up, and hauled my and Simone's butts to the principal's office. As soon as we saw that door looming at the end of the hallway, I offered Simone a deal. "Let's just say we were friends and we were only pretend fighting."

"OK, whatever," she said, and we walked in to meet the principal holding hands.

Well, Principal Drayton bought it, and after a brief talking-to about the dangers of playing too rough, she dismissed us. Rather than being united by our near-detention experience, Simone's and my truce was over as soon as we were back out that door.

"Forget you," she said.

"Forget you," I said.

"Forget you, forgot you. Never thought about you!"

"Gimme a piece of paper and I'll write all about you."

Shame.

In retrospect, I know that the reason I was a bully at school was because I had an older brother at home. Older bros are notoriously gender neutral when it comes to sibling torture, and he wasn't gonna take it easy on me just 'cause I was a girl.

One day, my bro and I were home alone. I heard a crash in the kitchen, and then my brother started screaming. I went running into the kitchen as fast as I could (which, remember, wasn't very fast) and saw my brother standing over the sink with blood gushing out of his mouth.

I screamed and did exactly what Mama always told us to do in these kind of situations: I grabbed the phone and dialed 911.

Next thing I knew, my brother was on me, ripping the phone out of my hand and slamming it down. And the blood pouring out his mouth smelled distinctly like . . . sweet tomatoes.

Ketchup.

Well, now I was crying, and instead of laughing it off as a practical joke, he was yelling at me that we were gonna get in trouble. Not because *he* had tried to trick *me*, but because I had called 911.

I was powerless. I couldn't win.

So where did I get my power back?

On the playground, baby. At school, I was a queen and in control. As soon as I walked in the doors of that school, I felt powerful, and I was gonna treat people badly as fuel, because I knew I'd be powerless again at the end of the day. I was gonna get my kicks on that four-square court while I could. And I was über-satisfied about it.

So how the hell did I go from calling another girl fat to being the woman telling the world to kiss my fat ass? Well, for starters, I'd like to thank Simone for punching me and Mr. Cosby for standing by while I got my butt kicked.

It wasn't too long after this that my superawkward skinny phase hit, and I found myself on the other side of bullying. I became the freak, the odd girl out, and the kid other kids knew they could pick on. That happened to coincide with a time when the Ethiopian famine was one of the top stories in the news, and because kids can be cruel—and uncreative as hell—they thought it was real funny to bring this up all the time. They'd come up at lunch and form a circle around me, holding hands and singing "We Are the World." I'd try to laugh it off, and I'd push my way out of the circle, all the while wanting to punch each and every one of them in the face. Not just for my sake but for all the children in Africa who really didn't have enough to eat.

But am I bitter about the fact that I was bullied?

Not at all.

I am grateful. I thank God that this happened, because I got to feel firsthand what I was doing to all those other girls.

But I am not condoning bullying. Bullying is a huge problem in the world that we live in now. One in three kids in the United States has been bullied at school, and more than three out of four have been bullied online (not surprising. Have you been on that thing called the Internet? It gets real mean, real fast). Selena Gomez, my girl Miley Cyrus, Jessica Alba, and my semi-doppelgänger (and fellow fivehead sista) Rihanna (love you, boo) have all talked about how they were bullied as kids and teenagers, and antibullying days are recognized around the world.

We all know about *Mean Girls*, but the Regina Georges of the world don't just vanish after high school: More than half of women have experienced bullying at work, and most of it from other women! It seems like the very sisters who should be helping you climb that ladder a couple of rungs are actually stomping on your knuckles, hoping you'll lose your grip and fall off.

You know I am not making this stuff up.

Check this out: Women, like all minority groups, experience something called tokenism. Have you heard of that before? It's when the power people make a feeble, fake stab at diversity and call it a day. (E.g., "We got one black dude, two women, and an Asian guy. We're very multicultural," says the CEO of a company with three hundred people.) When tokenism occurs, especially in high-stress work environments, rather than binding together and finding strength in numbers, we start competing and tryna pick each other off. When we are made to see each other as competition, we, well . . . we friggin' compete. It's human nature. And then, we all lose. When we come together, we win and we win big. Women and girls are safer together. We kick more butt, we make more dollars, we say #MeToo, we shout "Time's up," we make a bigger difference, and we send that patriarchy packing. We are a force to be reckoned with, and we are just getting started. Sisters before misters, shes before hes, Anns before Dans, chicks before d— . . . Lemme stop. You get it.

7

EMBRACE YOUR BEAUTY

Carolyn: When Tyra popped out of me, I took one look at her and thought, "This child is not mine."

Why?

Well, she opened her eyes and these big gray irises stared up at me like something out of *Rosemary's Baby*, or for you younger folks, *Gremlins*, or for you even younger folks, *American Horror Story*. "What kind of little alien is this?" I'd never seen eyes like that before, and had no idea where the heck they'd come from, but she'd been in my belly, so I knew that this was my martian. I mean, baby.

From the time in the delivery room when she first opened her mouth and started squawking, all anybody wanted to talk about was "those eyes." In our community, it's often considered a prize to have eyes that are anything other than cocoa brown, and everywhere we took that baby, people were falling all over themselves to comment on them. "She got some pretty eyes! Oh my God, look at *those eyes!*"

They acted like her daddy and I had something to be celebrated for, like we'd picked those eyes out of an IKEA box and installed them in her head ourselves. I didn't know what to say. Yes, I thought my daughter was special, but not because of those darn eyes.

Tyra: My eyes turned green as I got older, but I know exactly what Mama thought when she wanted to put sunglasses on my toddler self so that everyone would stop talking 'bout those eyes.

I'm having the same experience now with my son, who has the same big gray baby eyes that I did. And everywhere we go, that's the first thing people say about him. "Whoa, those eyes!" they exclaim. "Oh my God, look at *those eyes!*" (Well, first they say he looks just like his mama, because he does!)

Yeah, I think my baby is the most beautiful baby I have ever seen. He's the most gorgeous just because he is mine. If he was born with peepers the color of warm brownies, he would be my beautiful, bouncing (a lot! That boy loves to jump and climb!) baby boy. I want him to be so much more than "that boy wit' them pretty eyes."

So yeah, Ma, I now know exactly what you were going through. You still got those baby sunglasses?

Carolyn: Outside our house, lil adolescent TyTy continued to hear all about her damn eyes.

Every. Damn. Day.

But at home, we didn't talk about it. It wasn't that we wanted her to feel bad about the way she looked; it was the opposite: We wanted her to know that she was so much more than how she looked. Instead of complimenting her eyes, I complimented her dance moves, her crazy jokes and crazier facial expressions, and her self-guided focus when she was doing her homework. (Mama never had to tell her to get off that damn phone and open that social studies book.) We talked about how important it is to be a hard worker and a leader, someone people respect.

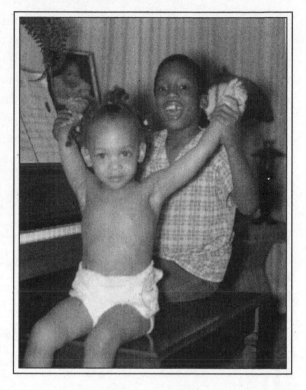

When Tyra was a tot, no one would shut up about her light green eyes! Now, York has the same eyes, and people won't stop talking about his peepers either!

👁 👁 *Tyra:* So back to this eye thing. People spend so much time talking about color—blue, green, hazel, lavender—but they fail to real-eyes it's also about eye shape, length and thickness of eyelashes, how your eyebrows frame your eyes, and even the size of the iris. So whether you have eyes that are light-colored or are an awesome shape like Jasmine's from *Aladdin,* when "You're so pretty/so beautiful/so gorgeous/so perfect [ugh]" is the go-to compliment for little girls, then they start thinking that's their sole worth. Whether I was getting complimented on my eyes or I was crying about how unhappy I was with my rail-thin body, my mama never made me feel like my true value was wrapped up in my outer package.

Carolyn: Even when Tyra went into an industry that was all about the physical, I tried to keep that from being my go-to compliment. Instead of saying, "Girl, you was looking good up on that catwalk!" I'd say, "I love what you did with your arms and smile at the end of the runway in that Todd Oldham show," or I'd compliment her on how well she'd negotiated a modeling contract. I didn't let her buy into the idea that a model is just a pretty face. "A model is a self-employed businesswoman, Ty," I'd say. "So you better be able to sashay that runway *and* take care of your business all day every day."

CREATIVE COMPLIMENTS

I often called out unusual things that proved how smart and funny Tyra was. This way, I made sure she knew that I was paying attention to the things that made her her, and not just the way she did her hair or the pretty dress she wore. Sure, I'd call her out for getting good grades, working hard, or being kind to other people, but I'd also compliment the quirky stuff. Such as:

➤ **HER HANDWRITING:** Put a pen in Tyra's hand and what you'll see is on point. Her handwriting looks like art, but it didn't start that way. Brandlie Garvey, a supersmart girl in Tyra's elementary school, had the best handwriting, so perfect it looked like a font, and Tyra got jealous. Real jealous. This prompted her to take a calligraphy class in high school (high school! Brandlie haunted her for years!), and after that, I was always asking her to write anything . . . the grocery list, you name it. "Dang, you got some good, fancy, Old English-lookin' handwriting, Tyra!" I'd tell her when she signed our Christmas cards.

➤ **HER DANCE MOVES:** Tyra can move and groove and twist and drop it really well. She didn't pick up all the new, cool dances immediately, but when she finally got them, she was a master: the Cabbage Patch, the Robocop, the Wop, the Running Man; she could bust a move. I'll never forget the time she went to an MC Hammer concert and was dancing so hard a crowd gathered to chant her on. By the end of the song, her strapless bra was around her waist and the entire stadium witnessed it on the Jumbotron.

➤ **BEING A PARROT:** Whatever accent she hears, she can repeat it exactly. When in Italy, she appears to be the chocolate girl who was born there to a Senegalese momma and Italiano pappa. France? You'd swear she was from Paris and chilled on the Champs-Élysées every damn day. Jamaica? Mon, she got that patois down. You bet g'yal from Montego Bay. It was uncanny and never failed to make me laugh. Of course, she also figured out that her talent with accents could help her underage butt sneak into clubs, but that's a story for another day.

👁 👁 *Tyra:* Girls who only hear about how pretty they are become women who are insanely terrified of losing their looks. They're even more scared of aging because their beauty has been presented to them as their most valuable asset. I know some women in the entertainment biz who are so pressed they've got their publicist going into Wikipedia to change their birth dates to make 'em a few years (or a decade) younger. Imagine this: A PR intern comes in every morning, fires up the computer, and sips his Stumptown while he rolls back the ages of their clients.

But can you blame the age adapters? Hell no. We as a society have told them that once Ms. Aging rears her head, the expiration dates are about to start poppin' off:

> The desire for women as lovers: gone.

> The desire for women as entertainers: over.

> The desire for women as professionals: in the past.

> The perception of women as beautiful: sayonara.

> The perception of women as valuable: so yesterday.

> The perception of women as interesting: the end.

We tell them all the good parts of life will all go away. Just poof and disappear. So no wonder we women think of aging as the big, bad bogeyman, coming to wreck your boobs, your forehead, your butt, your eyes, your neck, your thighs, your smile, and your life.

What would happen if we celebrated getting older (and not just once a year with a cake and some candles) instead of trying to pretend it wasn't happening?

I'm in my forties, and while I have a tendency to look younger than my years, does my ass look the same as it did when I was twenty? My face is preserved well (you know the saying, and yeah, I will admit: it don't crack). But my body?

Hahahahahahahahahahaha—no.

Each thigh and bun has about twenty more cellulite dimples. I think I'm averaging about one new dimple a year, too. And I no longer pass the booty pencil test. (Ask a friend if you don't know what that is.) But how many effs do I give about that? Zero. Well, maybe two. I do wish my lower body was more toned, and I go to the gym sometimes to do something about it, but not enough because I honestly don't care enough. It's drooping because of my age, but I ain't *trippin'* about my age.

And I know it's cuz my mama couldn't give a damn about hers.

Carolyn: Who wants to be young and dumb their whole life? Embracing your age means embracing your experience. It means you've learned from all your stupid mistakes and you aren't gonna make 'em again. Every year that goes by, I also get to say whatever the heck I wanna say more and more. I just let it rip! (Not farts, mind you; I'm talking about honesty, although aging does make it difficult to hold those gas explosions in at will.) I used to care so much about what other people thought about me, but I care less and less with every year that goes by. Getting older means doing and saying whatever the heck you want to do, no matter who (not even your bigmouthed daughter) tells you to stop.

For instance, Tyra and I eat out a lot, and there is usually some type of finger food on the table—barbecue ribs, pizza, fried

Believe it or not, my mama
and I are the same age in
each of these photos—sixteen!

chicken, veggies and ranch dressing—'cause we love anything you can eat with your hands. Don't you think it tastes better? Only problem is that even when something's finger-lickin' good, unlike Tyra, I'm not one to be licking my fingers. I don't know why, really, but I just don't do it. So I just eat and eat, and my fingers get sticky and nasty, and my hands get stickier and nastier. Then, at the end of the meal, I wash 'em in my water glass. Yep, right at the table of a three-star Michelin-rated restaurant, I just plunge my hands right down in there, and if there's ice, even better—I'll use it like soap. Then I'll use my napkin to dry my hands. It's my cleansing system.

This totally grosses out Tyra, to the point where she makes gagging noises. And to top off her disdain, I leave a glass on the table swirling with pizza grease, chicken skin, and barbecue bits (or caviar if it's one of those fancy-shmancy places). As she puts it, it looks like "watery throw-up." I'm sixty-nine years old—I don't care if other people are watching me! And I don't care if I gross out my child. If Gordon Ramsay saw me, he would curse me out, throw me out of his restaurant, and toss my "sink" water at my head. I'd just come back the next day and do it all over again, GR. Only problem is that now my two-year-old grandson thinks this looks like so much fun, so he does it, too!

Sorry, Mama TyTy (not).

Tyra: Yes, York now does this, and it grinds my nerves that he learned it from his grandmom. But I have to admit, it does beat having to get up and haul him to the ladies' room to wash his hands. And don't tell my mom, but when she's not looking, I may or may not dip my greasy hands in, too.

Carolyn: Now, some people say I look kinda young for my age. And I'll admit it, I do. But there's one thing I do to show the world that I have lived one incredible life: I don't dye my hair (sorry, Clairol). I love my gray hair, but when I first started getting those wisps of wisdom growing out of my scalp, I felt all self-conscious about it because people were always pointing it out. "Wow, Carolyn, your hair is going gray. Why don't you cover it?"

So I marched my butt down to the salon, where my stylist was skeptical. "Are you for real?" she asked. "Do you know how much work that is going to take to maintain? And I know you ain't a high-maintenance woman."

But I insisted, so she did it. I went home, took one look at my jet-black hair in the mirror. I didn't look like myself at all, so I marched my butt right back to the salon, where the stylist was just waiting for me, shaking her head. "I can't strip it," she said. "You're gonna have to cut it."

So I said good-bye to my phony black hair and let the gray grow in. It's my crown of silver, and I'm damn proud of it. There's a story that goes along with each strand: Some of 'em came from my marriages, some from Tyra's modeling agents, some from when she signed me up for online dating unbeknownst to me, and some from Tyra's foolishness herself. These icy strands represent the insane amount of work I've put in and the crazy lessons I've learned (many you're reading in this book!)—why the hell would I want to hide that? I have no time to pretend I'm still young and dumb. And hell, even with all the money in the world, you couldn't pay me to be twenty again. (Except for hot flashes. I'd pay somebody to make those disappear. Just tell me who to make the check out to.)

For many women, it's the complete opposite, and there are twenty-year-olds out there who are hightailing it to the salon and paying top dollar to get their silver fox on. I'll be interested to see if they keep the gray when it really starts sprouting from their scalps!

Over the years with *Top Model*, I'd occasionally visit the set to give the contestants pep talks or offer support, but one of my favorite times that Tyra had me appear on the show was in cycle 22, when she asked me to photograph the final four contestants—with their mothers.

First off, I was shaking on set because it'd been so long since I'd been a professional photographer, but once I got that camera in my hands, it was like riding a bike—it all came back to me!

All the contestants had unique relationships with their mothers, and seeing them reunited was emotional for everyone involved. At the beginning of the shoot, all the moms were very uncomfortable in front of the camera, and one even broke down in tears when she saw herself all fierced up! I had to work to get those mamas to open up, let go, and just flow. I had to remind them that they were beautiful and just as worthy as their young'uns!

When Tyra revealed the final photos, everyone was in tears, even the crew! One of the models, a grown man, almost fell to his knees crying so hard when he saw how stunning his mother looked in those photographs. I really thought that when you looked at those pictures, you could tell exactly what each contestant's mother meant to them.

👁 👁 *Tyra:* Props to my mama, and all those mamas, because those were some of the most beautiful and deep photographs I've ever seen on *Top Model*!

And I wasn't the only one who thought that—when we posted about them on social media, the response was emotional and overwhelming. Everyone loved seeing the moms all edgy and glammed up. When they saw those photos, they weren't seeing age; they were just seeing pure beauty and the mother-child bond.

It wasn't too long after that when I decided to ditch the age limit for *Top Model* contestants. In cycle 24 (yes, 24 baby, we been around!), I welcomed our oldest contestant yet—a drop-dead-fierce mama (who's a grandmama, too!) who had decided to finally devote herself to her modeling dreams after spending two decades raising her beautiful family. People were to' up from the flo' up with tears and excitement seeing me give her a chance at her dream that got deferred. The outpouring of support and tons of love she got was tremendous. Clearly, I wasn't the only one out here ready to see some mother hens up on the runway with all them spring chickens!

And Mama's dedication to her own gray hair is rare and next-level fierce! There are some famous mamas out there who look really good. Their hair is laid, it looks stupendous, and there's no gray. And I'll admit, they look slammin'. So back in the day when I took my mom to my fave wig shops to find her a version of these cool mom hairdos, she yelled . . .

 Carolyn: That ain't me!

 Tyra: And she yelled it hella loud.

 Carolyn: Even with a wig, I want to look like myself. I want a lovely silver-colored wig that still represents my

Tyra and I switched wigs and expressions after a J.Lo show in Las Vegas. How's my Smize?

acceptance of my age. It ain't easy, though: Gray wigs that don't make you look like the little church lady in the front pew are darn hard to find!

👁️ 👁️ *Tyra:* Yes they are. Mama'll have me going from wig store to wig store in Chicago, Atlanta, New York, and Paris(!) searching for some salt and pepper.

👄 *Carolyn:* So when I do find stylish ones, no matter where I am, I buy them in bulk.

👁️ 👁️ *Tyra:* It is easy being stuck in customs and explaining that she's not planning to sell these bundles of wigs back in America. Why? They take one look at all that gray swimming in her carry-on and know not many American women would want to touch them with a ten-foot pole!

👄 *Carolyn:* I have to say, the only thing that did surprise me about aging was the gravitational pull. I remember the first time I noticed it, looking in the mirror. "Hmm," I thought, "things that used to be standing up are now lying down." Then eventually, they weren't just lying down; they were looking at the floor!

I went to the store and bought every kind of breast lifter, tummy tucker, and butt smoother I could find, but squeezing myself into them just reminded me of when my own mama tried to make me wear a girdle. It triggered something in my brain: Instead of making me feel better and more beautiful, all those stretchy tubes made me feel bad about myself. To hell with this. If a saggy body is what getting older is, then I'll take it. 'Cause this is me.

👁️ 👁️ *Tyra:* Sorry, Ma. I have to disagree with you here. I love me some stretchy-ass tubes, and most women do. After all, God created Adam, Eve, and Sara Blakely so that she could create Spanx.

👄 *Carolyn:* Well, while you sit there and can't breathe, let me finish what the heck I was saying. Physical beauty . . . it's just a shell, baby. I know we have all met people who had a Hershey's Kiss sparkly, pretty wrapper of a face and body, but when you got to know them, they "tasted" like a vomit-flavored Jelly Belly (yeah, those really exist). When outer beauty is all you've got and you're not intelligent or kind, people will get tired of your crap real fast. You'll even get tired of yourself. Wrappers, no matter how pretty, eventually get crumpled up and thrown away (and no amount of smoothin' makes them look new again).

So yes, Tyra modeled and got lots of success for her exterior features. But I know full well that what made her into a supermodel wasn't the forehead and the boobs, but the brain and heart behind 'em.

MY GREEN-EYED MONSTER

Now, don't get me wrong—I do occasionally get a lil bit jealous of the younger models. Because . . . TECHNOLOGICAL ADVANCES!

KENDALL JENNER: You can be anywhere in the world and FaceTime with your mama! I had to share a landline with ten other girls in New York City, or walk down the street and around the corner to the pay phone in Paris every time I wanted to talk to mine.

GIGI HADID: You've never had to navigate a map the size of a tablecloth to get to a fitting. You have GPS!

BELLA HADID: You have Uber and Lyft! You don't have to stand in the rain in New York City, trying to hail a cab to take you crosstown at five p.m. in the middle of fashion week.

JOURDAN DUNN: You don't have to mix four shades of foundation from three different brands to achieve your color match. There are actually a decent amount of cosmetics companies that now have a myriad of shades to match most brown girls' skin tones!

KARLIE KLOSS: You don't have to wait until interviews to prove you're smart as a whip. Your fans see it every day on your social media feeds! Oh, you can also set the record straight yourself whenever the tabloids start spoutin' a bunch of lies.

8

FIX IT
OR FLAUNT IT

Tyra: On the Victoria's Secret runway, I was always covering my ass.

You may think I'm referring to watching out for nasty models who wanted to trip me on the runway because my Angel wings were bigger than theirs. But no. The VS models were a family, so there was none of that *Showgirls* cray-cray going on.

I'm talking about literally covering my ass.

In the beginning, this would just be a little bloop of a skirt that dipped down over my upper thighs. Later, when the Angel costumes became elaborate and thematic, it might be a flowing Princess Diana wedding dress train, a floor-length feather coat, or a sheer flamenco skirt to the floor, but I made sure I always got a little extra. Some of the models strutted their stuff in a thong, nothing more than a few little rhinestones above their crack (and more power to them), but the thought of doing that had my tummy rumbling and my feet quaking in my heels.

I was proud of the fact that I had a good twenty pounds (at least) on every other model up there. I loved my body, and having a little jiggle with my wiggle made me different. What I wasn't so proud of was my dimples.

Dimples on your face: cute. Dimples on my butt: not so much.

My cellulite was stubborn as a mule (and I'm not talking about those backless, closed-toed shoes). It was completely independent of my weight—no matter how much I gained or lost, my cellulite was still there. So I had to learn to deal.

And by deal, I mean hide that ish.

Heading to the beach? Don't let me forget my sarong. Dating a new man? Well, for the first six months, I'll just walk backward when I get up out of bed. I don't want him to look over in the morning, as the first rays of sun hit my cottage cheese thighs, and think, "Dang! I thought she was a supermodel! What the hell is all that?"

Almost every woman has an Achilles' heel when it comes to body confidence, whether it's her cankles, bingo wings, turkey necks, thunder thighs, or muffin tops, and mine just happens to be my bumpy butt. I loved me some *Wonder Woman* TV episodes when I was a little girl, and it didn't seem like she found any flaws when she looked in the mirror, but most of us are not Amazonian warrior princesses who can fight dudes with a bow and arrow better than Robin Hood and his hood. (But who knows? Maybe every once in a while, Diana catches her rear view and thinks, "Ugh. Just for once, couldn't I save the world in a maxi skirt? Or at least some friggin' loose-fitting culottes?" Naw. I met today's Wonder Woman, Gal Gadot, recently, and on top of being sweet as pecan pie, she was in friggin' *wonder*ful shape.) We mortal chicks, though, usually zero in on one or two things we don't like. But I say don't obsess about it.

Fix it or flaunt it.

Carolyn: When I was a teenager, the in thing was having a teeny-tiny waist. Now, I was not a teeny-tiny girl. I had a six-pack tummy, but when I put on my gym uniform, my thighs bulged out from my shorts like a couple of water balloons, but it never bothered me all that much.

It bothered my mother, though, even though they weren't her thighs or her belly. She was always trying to get me to wear a girdle. And not just trying—she'd *make* me. Now, I love me some period dramas, but this wasn't *The Age of Innocence* or *Downton Abbey*. It was the 1960s, when everyone was dancing the swim and the mashed potato, but Mama had retro values and rocked a girdle on her skinny frame daily, so she made me tug that panty girdle up until it was so tight around my middle that I woulda surely passed out if I set one foot on the dance floor, much less tried to mash a darn potato. Then she'd make me top it off with a big wide belt, like squeezin' the hell out of my middle was just my style. But no amount of Mama's cinching gave me a skinny waist, so finally, I took that girdle off one day at school and threw it in the trash.

When I told my mother what I'd done, she was pissed, with a capital *P*. She accused me of wasting good, hard-earned money, but I stood my ground. I told her she could keep on buying me girdles if that was what she wanted, but I'd just keep throwin' 'em in the trash. I wasn't about to risk fainting every day or waste away for no damned waist.

👁 👁 *Tyra:* I didn't know I had a *five*head until I became a model. Yep, my frontal lobe was just normal to me, until people started to know my name everywhere I went.

First came the fame, then came the forehead jokes. Shoot, the rapper the Game even busted some lyrics about it. Everyone wants to be mentioned in a rap song—it's, like, the ultimate nod of love—but maybe not when said rapper uses the space between your eyebrows and your hairline to dis you *and* Mariah Carey in one line. Then flash-forehead-forward a few years, and I just loved seeing that black man blush crimson when he was guesting on *Top Model*. He could hardly look me in the eye when I questioned him about the "forehead like Tyra" verse. (Mariah, just hit me up if you want me to guest on a battle reply to homeboy.)

My friend Raphael Saadiq of Tony! Toni! Toné! fame still calls me Tweety Bird whenever he sees me. I like to think it's cuz I have big eyes like that cartoon canary, but we all know the nickname is probably inspired by the region above my eyes. The flip side of this was that my forehead was as much a part of my secret model's arsenal as my arse. (And, like I always say: The bigger the forehead, the bigger the brain.)

If I wanted to look edgy and high fashion, I could slick my hair back and put my forehead on full blast. Throw a little intimidation in my Smize and I was an ice queen from the future come to stomp on all y'all. Or I could put my Tweety away by adding a clip-on bang, and look like an approachable, all-American sweetheart on her way to someone's sweet sixteen bash. *I tawt I taw a big forehead. I did—I did taw a big forehead!*

Instead of a flaw that kept me from getting work, my fivehead turned out to be an advantage, my own sweetest taboo (shout out to that gorgeous goddess of a chanteuse Sade, my sister from another big-foreheaded mister). Why? Because it gave me a *Vogue* today, Victoria's Secret tomorrow versatility that most models of my time didn't have.

(Maybe I shoulda looked into getting it insured—have someone in a suit from Allstate come out and measure it. Is it too late, Dennis Haysbert?)

However, the truth: If someone would have come to me when I was first teased about my forehead and offered me the option of forehead reduction surgery, would I have forged my mama's signature on the papers then and there?

Who knows?

Actually . . .

Naw.

Carolyn: Big-forehead gene is in our DNA. I have one, my father has one, and Tyra's just carrying on our proud heritage. Luckily, Tyra wasn't insecure about her forehead, because I always encouraged her to wear her hair slicked back in a bun.

Just two big-forehead women havin' a bangin' good time.

My personal hairstyle has always been the slicked-back chignon, and I tend to think the bigger the forehead, the better the slick-back. Just add some oil or gel, brush a lil baby hair down around those edges, and you're rhet ta go, forehead shining bright like a diamond (OK, pat it with a lil loose powder), on full display for all to see. Over the years, and because of a few mishaps with lye-based straighteners (long story; I'm sure a lot of you have been there yourself), my frontal lobe has grown as my hairline has thinned. While the world is teasing my baby on the daily about her fivehead, Mama will continue to embrace her own, even if it someday goes all the way back to my ears.

Fiveheads: If ya got 'em, flaunt 'em!

Tyra: Let's be real, though. Learning to love the thing you hate (or have been teased about) can't always be done. We are humans with emotions, feelings, societal pressures, and social media (!), and there are some things we will always just not like.

And that's OK. It really is.

So I say, if you can't figure out a way to flaunt it, then you totally have a right to fix it.

For example: I tweaked my nose. I had a Pinocchio nose: It just kept growing. Though instead of growing long, it continued to grow left and right in the area between my eyes. And that spot felt itchy all the time. Like the skin was stretching or something.

Besides the itching, I didn't have an issue with my nose, but when I started modeling, someone else did. A super blunt makeup artist said, "Girl," as I sat in her chair while she blushed my cheeks. "There's something weird going on with your nose. Those nose bones . . . I swear they're bigger than last year. You ever thought about getting that fixed? It's like it's alive."

When I was little, about three years old, I fell hard on my face while my aunt was babysitting me. "Carolyn, you need to take this baby to the hospital," she said when Mama came to pick me up. "She broke her nose!"

Well, I wasn't screaming and crying that much, so Mama wasn't having it, so no hospital trip for me. But all those years later, we started to wonder if maybe my aunt had been right, and that part of why my upper nose bones were growing so funky had to do with my tipsy toddler tumble.

Out of curiosity, I made an appointment with a doctor. He was highly regarded, and he examined me and said my nose was a medical, mangled mess and needed a complete overhaul. He proceeded to make all of these high-tech sketches of what my newly conceived nose would look like. It was straight-up-too-thin-too-pointy-too-WTF. I was like "Nose way, José."

Awhile later, I heard about another respected doctor. But this one seemed to have a bit more respect for the truth. He said that my upper nose bones did seem quite askew, and confirmed that the itching was because of the offish direction of growth, but that there was absolutely no medical need to fix it. My breathing was fine. He told me he could stop the itching and sculpt my nose with his philosophy—to preserve ethnic features.

Did he keep his physical promise and did the itching stop? You nose it.

But I was pretty "meh" about Mama's attempt at fixing something.

Carolyn: Are you talking about when I got them fillers on my laugh lines?

Tyra: You know it.

Carolyn: After all those needles, I looked the damn same!

Tyra: She did! You couldn't tell one bit! And when I asked her why she did it, she said, "Well, all these women my age are doing it, so why not?" But she already looked young! So I got to be the mama that day. "If all your friends were jumping off the Brooklyn Bridge, would you jump, too?" I asked. "'Cause that was a waste of your dang dollars!"

But usually I'm all for women doing whatever they want to do, because let's face it, natural beauty is unfair.

I'll say it again. Natural beauty is friggin' unfair.

Yeah, I said it again. It's pure luck.

Think about it: If someone becomes a multimillionaire by running into a twenty-four-hour mart drunk to buy some more malt liquor and a winning scratch card, are you going to praise him for his financial acumen and hard work? Hell no! You will shake your head and think, "Dang, he's got some good-ass luck!" Or would you praise someone who was born a prince in a gilded castle complete with servants whose jobs are to wash his royal behind for working his way up the ranks (unless he was bootstrapping his way up from that first job in the castle mail room or fetching the queen her cappuccino)? Again, can I get a hell, no?

So why praise a naturally beautiful woman and say she's good at life? Let's face it—it's not like she worked for that natural beauty. Her parents just rolled the dice with some sperm and an egg and came up with doubles. Luck, boo. Pure luck. I was born with some good genes (thanks, Daddy, for these long legs), but I am not a "natural" beauty.

Now, I'm going to pause a minute while you Google "Tyra Banks no makeup."

Did ya do it?

Oh yeah, I see you're laughing. You did it.

I'm just two big eyes and a forehead, right? (Or maybe two eyes and four foreheads.) That's the real me, but I got a few (like in the hundreds) tricks up my sleeve. If I was a superhero (Tyzonia,

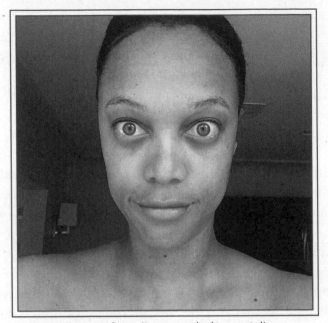

Me + no makeup = You can see why this went viral!

me and Diana/Gal would be homies), my power would be posing and finding the right light. So, if a giant meteor was heading right for New York City, y'all could call me (just flash your makeup mirror a couple of times) and I would be there in a jiffy. Not to save your butts, of course, just to show you how to make sure the glow from all the explosions hits your good side and that you don't have a double chin when that bridge goes down. Once I get myself all done up, I look bangin' and I know it. But Tyzonia did not #wokeuplikethis. Nope. #ittakesavillage.

Me + lotsa makeup = You wanna ask me for Tyover tips, dontcha?

Carolyn: That was one of the first things I tried to teach Tyra back when she was struttin' the living room in my nightgown and heels, prepping for Paris: It wasn't just about how she looked standin' there straight outta bed, but how she could transform.

One of the things that makes Tyra so unique is her facial

expressions. She can look chic and glamorous, but she can also look like she belongs on *SNL*. She must have about thirty-seven more muscles in her face than the rest of us. When she really wants to turn it up a notch, she can contort them until she looks buck-wild crazy (I swear she isn't, though).

She's a chameleon. Whatever you want her to be, she can be. So when I see her transform, it's kind of spectacular. I look at her like, "Wow, I created a princess? A doll? A tiger? A gazelle? A mermaid?" And then she makes a crazy face and I think, "A fool. I created a fool."

Chameleon Tyra still
blows my mind!

👁 👁 *Tyra:* Any model who thinks she's got a one-way ticket to the top just because of her natural beauty has another thing coming. Natural beauty may get you about two steps up the stairway to success, but then you gotta work.

But who could blame a woman for thinking natural beauty is something to bank on? So many people reward natural beauty with power, so oftentimes, cookie-cutter beauties get all sorts of perks, from more money in their jobs to rich men who want to take care of them. Studies have shown that women who are perceived as more attractive make 5 percent more at work and even get higher grades in school. So, are we going to say that beautiful women are more intelligent and better employees, or that the world has a discriminatory bias? My money's on the bias, baby, even though it's hardly ever acknowledged. But I think that's changing as we speak. In a 2017 *Allure* essay called "Being Pretty Is a Privilege, but We Refuse to Acknowledge It," Janet Mock wrote about how we live in a culture that says a woman's looks are her worth. And that "pretty" people *do* get special treatment, and that we need to take some ownership of that. That there is favoritism everywhere based on how people look. Janet went on to say that beauty isn't something she worked super hard for, but that her looks have helped her journey big-time.

I smacked the table and yelled hallelujah when I read that!

She damn near blew my mind, because she was articulating so many thoughts I'd had over the years and blowing open a whole new conversation. These are *exactly* the kinds of things we need to talk about when we talk about beauty, especially as we (and when I say "we," I mean society—from tabloids to television shows, social media, and online commenters) love to look down on women who try to make themselves more beautiful so that they can get a little bit of that same privilege and power.

"Oh my God, did you see her? What the hell does she think she's doing? She got so much surgery, that's awful." Yeah, her surgery may look a bit, ummm . . . overdone. But, come on—we gotta be real and admit our society did that to her. It does it to all of us in some way. (I write this as I am getting a floor-length weave sewn in.) Shoot, man . . . I know as a model I represented a look that was pretty intimidating, and I would go overboard to dispel the myths of perfection.

As more and more women (and men) embrace the beautification tools that are available to them, and those tools become easier and easier to use (it's not too inconceivable to think that soon we'll be rolling through the drive-through to get some cheek implants with our iced blueberry decaf green tea mocha quinoa unicorn Pegasus framboozles), I think that we'll see big shifts in the perception of beauty.

Carolyn: If you want proof of how much the perception of beauty changes in just a few decades, look no further than my high school pictures! Tyra loves to tease me and say that I looked fifteen going on thirty-five, but everybody did in the '60s! Helmet hair was all the rage back then, and hell, if we could stand outside in the wind and it didn't ruffle a single strand, then we thought our bangs looked bangin'!

👁 👁 *Tyra:* Mama's right—beauty has already shifted to a much more undone state than it was in her day. No one was rocking beach waves and BB cream at her high school graduation—it was all about the bouffants and lashes so solid they cast a shadow.

I think that in the future, the most prized looks will be the flawsome ones (flaws + awesome ones), not the perfect ones. Then you might have people lining up to get their ears tweaked to stick out because that connotes youth, or wearing contacts to turn their blue eyes to dark brown; people will be using darkening creams to bring out their freckles and cocoa-deep skin, and dentists will make millions specializing in creating strategic imperfections. Who knows? I mean, shoot—in the Renaissance times, people used to go out of their way to turn their low foreheads into fiveheads! People were putting themselves through pain to achieve my lobe by plucking or pulling out their hair!

I wish I could create my very own time capsule of the non-cookie-cutter beauty trends that I see coming and stuff them in that box today and then five hundred years from now, someone opens it and announces to the world that I was right.

The one thing I do know is that the world's perception of beauty is constantly changing. Trying to keep up and adapt to what everyone else thinks is beautiful is so damn tiring. I'm tired just writing about it. One year we are supposed to have a small butt. Years later, it should be gargantuan and lookin' like that peach emoji (🍑). Big boobs are all the rage. Oops, now a flat chest and no bra is what women crave. Thick brows are what everyone wants! Wait, what's that? Oh, you plucked them bare a couple of years ago, when everyone wanted brows that looked like they were drawn on with a pencil, and now they won't grow

Backstage, no makeup, right in the middle of the skinny eyebrow trend! #90s

back? Well, too bad for you. Or how about that time you dropped some lye bills at the salon, only to have someone later that day tell you relaxed hair is so last year, all the cool girls are going natural now, and honey, a '70s Afro would look so cute on you! So you just sit there and smile, thinking about your empty wallet and how it all makes you so frustrated you could eat your hot comb.

Carolyn: Curvylicious is definitely more of a trend today than it was when high fashion told Tyra to take a hike (and that was when we hiked ourselves over to the pizza place), and I love seeing modeling embrace bigger girls like Precious Lee and Saffi Karina (not to mention Tyra's girl Ashley Graham).

But I'll also always respect the thin girls, because that was Tyra at one time, too. I always wanted her to feel good about herself no matter what size her body was demanding it be at that moment. Mama Carolyn loves her baby girl, and every woman round this world, through thick, thin, and in between.

Tyra: Don't get hung up on natural versus unnatural beauty, 'cause the end result is all the same—your reflection should make you Smize because you look just how you want to look. When it comes to beauty, it ain't where ya from; it's where ya at.

What matters most is that you feel like you are good enough. Maybe you hate makeup and think you look best with just a little tinted moisturizer! You go. Maybe you don't want to leave your house without a full-face contour and some serious eyebrow microblading. You go, too!

As women, we have to be careful, because there are all sorts of unseen enemies out there lurking (and sometimes, this enemy is sitting at your dining room table, eating food that you cooked), trying to make you think that you are not enough and that feeling beautiful is reserved for those other women, women who are not anything like you. There are other types of enemies who will go on and on about how you look better without makeup, when what they really mean is they don't want you looking and feeling your best because they are scared to lose you ('cause your bright red lips and chiseled-contoured cheeks were what caught their eye in the first place). You gotta watch out for this type and learn to recognize the signs ("What's that crap all over your face?") so that when you come across any of these frenemies, you can just poke 'em in the eye with your mascara wand. (I mean that figuratively, not literally!) They are not worth your time or lip liner.

It is unrealistic to expect to feel 100 percent good about yourself 100 percent of the time. There will always be little things that you don't like or wish you could change, and those things will probably change from day to day. But don't spend too much time worrying about it. Fix it or flaunt it, then get on with it!

You and your flawsome self got sh*t to do!

I'M AT A PARTY, eating damn near all the snacks (yes to those tiny crab cakes!) and sipping on a cucumber mint lemonade when I spot a modeling agent I've known for years. I'm practically pulling my arm out of the socket waving at him, but when he finally does come over to say hi, he seems less than pleased to see me. In fact, he seems almost pissed.

"Tyra girl, I am so over you," he says.

"Oh my God, did they run out of crab cakes?"

He shakes his head and sips his vodka soda. "These open calls are running me ragged. We've got girls lining up at the agency at six a.m.—one of 'em even brought a lawn chair! All day, they just keep coming! We can't take a lunch, we can't schedule any meetings, we can't get any work done."

"Wow, that's bananas!" I say while snatching a spring roll. "But why you mad at me?"

I gotta admit, he does look weary, and if we were on a plane, those bags under his eyes would not fit under the seat.

"Because your ass is on *Top Model* every week, telling all these girls all over the world that they're all special and that they can be models and they believe you!" He signals the waiter

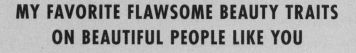

MY FAVORITE FLAWSOME BEAUTY TRAITS ON BEAUTIFUL PEOPLE LIKE YOU

- Freckles (obsessed)
- Frizzy hair
- Unibrows
- Bald heads
- A chipped front tooth
- Different-color eyes
- Eyes that are too far apart
- Very square heads
- Super-round faces
- Tiny boobies
- Fiveheads (I know, I am biased)
- Skin that is two (or more) different colors
- Being super tall
- Being super short
- A crooked smile
- A mole in the "wrong" place

for another vodka. "We used to have about seven girls a week show up for our open calls. Now we get hundreds. Last Thursday, it was so busy, all I ate all day was half a Luna bar I found in the trash." He shakes his head like today's the saddest day of his life. "And it was a lemon one, and I don't even like the lemon ones."

As I continue to stuff my face, he continues his diatribe. "So we are gonna stop walk-ins and just have them mail in pics or send them in online."

"So, let me get this straight," I say. *"America's Next Top Model* killed the open call because now there are thousands of girls out there who recognize their own beauty and feel that they could walk the runway or be on the cover of a magazine, too?"

"Yep," he says, jabbing a cocktail straw at me like it's a dagger. "And it's all your fault, bitch!"

Now, I'm tryna keep a smile off my face. Because it may be a problem for him that more women now consider themselves beautiful because of *Top Model*, but it's a major win for Tyzonia, the modeling profession, and the entire freakin' planet! Low self-esteem and lack of self-worth are plagues, and we have to eradicate them. Expanding what is considered beautiful in our culture is a huge leap in the right direction, and more of those atypical girls lining up for modeling agency open calls will get signed because of it (a.k.a. making an agent's job easier because he'll have more models to work with than ever before!). I want to keep pushing and keep blowing the beauty door open so that eventually, every woman feels like the idea of beauty applies to her in some way, shape, or form.

One of my favorite things about *Top Model* was taking the contestants' ideas of beauty and then putting 'em in the Vitamix until they were completely unrecognizable but just as tasty (if not even sweeter). Over the course of a cycle, I tried to get the girls to look beyond the traditional definitions of desirable that they'd been indoctrinated with since they were just tykes in their strollers, reaching for the blond-haired, blue-eyed baby doll. It is the most rewarding experience for me when a girl starts to embrace and flaunt the very things she once hated about herself.

One season of *Top Model*, we had a stunning model who had

skin the color of my mom's, which for African Americans is considered medium hued, but she said that where she's from, it's considered very dark. Dang, that girl was so unique and interesting-looking with that strong, square head shape I adore. She always wore light-colored contacts, and to the panel of judges, they stood out on her face not always in the best way. When I finally asked her about them, she said that she was taught that the darker you are, the more you need to attain stereotypical beauty in other ways.

I worked overtime to boost her confidence from week to week to show her just how special her reflection was. Finally, she appeared in the judging room one day without the contacts, and she had the most gorgeous cocoa-colored eyes. She told me that although she had not expected it, she had never felt more beautiful, or better about herself, than she did on *Top Model*.

When she said that, I had a hard time holding back my tears (and I had to learn to hold back my tears on *Top Model*, or I woulda just bawled my eyes out through each and every episode, and no one wants to watch twenty-four cycles of Tyra cryin'). Her words really touched me, and I felt for all my deeply hued sisters who have ever felt or heard anything negative about their skin color. I hope that they got a little bit of healing along with my model in that moment, and had a little (or a helluva lot) more appreciation for their skin color, no matter what stunning shade it was, the next time they stood in front of a mirror.

To this day, my *Top Model* casting team and I are obsessed with showcasing a myriad of skin tones on our show, from alabaster to butterscotch to ebony and everything in between. When my boy Lin-Manuel Miranda, the creator of *Hamilton*, accepted his Tony Award just hours after the deadly mass shooting at the gay club Pulse in Orlando, he recited a poem he had written about it. The line "And love is love is love is love is love is love is love is love . . ." hasn't left my brain since I heard it in that moment. It's a powerful reminder to accept love in its whole, true, pure form, and I like to mirror him by saying, "Beauty is beauty is beauty is beauty. . . ."

No slicing and dicing beauty into a series of rights and wrongs, greater-thans and less-thans. It just is.

Your beauty is beautiful.

WE ALL WANT WHAT WE DON'T HAVE

When I saw a girl standing in front of me wearing contact lenses to get my eye color, all I could think about was how my entire life, I have been surrounded by imagery and people saying her hair texture was the absolute ultimate. Dozens of wigs and weaves later, I still struggle with what was drilled into my head by society as a kid. Hair is very emotional for women and is oftentimes a political thing, too. Those struggles in my community, and many others, continue to this day.

When it comes to our reflections, the grass-colored eyeshadow is always greener in someone else's makeup caddy:

To name just a few:

➤ Girls with straight hair want curls and beachy waves, but curly girls get Brazilian blow-outs and no-lye relaxer treatments.

➤ Girls with unibrows don't leave home without their tweezers in tow, while the thin-browed

ladies will go down swinging to save their
eyebrow pencil.

➤ There are pale girls slathering on that bronzer
(way better than the tanning beds of the '80s and
'90s), while some darker-hued girls are investing
in lightening creams.

➤ The thin-lipped are getting injections to plump up
their pouts, while some with naturally bodacious
smackers are using plastic surgery to reduce theirs.
(Google it. The pictures are like . . . whoa!)

Carolyn: I love that, Ty. you're making Mama really
proud right now.

Tyra: Now's the time where you're probably
thinking, "So, Tyra, if you want to make the girls feel better about
themselves, and if you're all crying and boo-hooing over your
model's breakthrough, then why the heck are you giving them
makeovers every damn season?"

Well, I'm glad you asked, because, boo, I am not giving them
makeovers. I'm giving them Tyovers, and that's a whole different
type a thang.

The harsh truth that I found out as a young model is that not
every flaw can be flaunted in fashion.

This is especially true—and probably especially harsh—in the

Discussing Tyovers behind the scenes on *Top Model* with executive producer Jaimie Glasson.

world of modeling, where you are trying to build a career by selling your physicality and image to clients. Modeling takes real-world scrutiny and kicks it up ten notches. Hell, maybe even a hundred. And it's crazy because you may be pretty much OK with how you look but then get signed to a modeling agency and all of a sudden you're hearing all kinds of crazy stuff about yourself that you were *never* insecure about. Like, what the heck do you mean that my calves are not in proportion to my thighs or that my waist is too long to look good in a bikini or my belly button is odd cuz it's neither an innie nor an outie or that my profile is too flat or that when I smile my top lip disappears and I have to learn to smile not as real to keep the fullness in my upper lip? The industry needs to realize the power it wields with this kind of feedback. (Ummm . . . Mizz TyTy is the recipient of all those ummm . . . comments, BTW.)

Carolyn: When Tyra would hear those kinda things, she always took it like a pro. However, Mama was the one who'd start foaming at the mouth and looking around for something (or someone) to smack. Sometimes I'd have to excuse myself and go to the bathroom just to take a few breaths and calm down, 'cause I knew swiping an agent's desk and throwing all their stuff on the floor wasn't gonna help my baby get booked.

Tyra: It feels like those fashion biz powers that be in black are just hating on you hard, and they are—but in a different way. They're hating to lose money and wanting you to be as marketable as possible. So, they break it all down, and often break you down in the process. But yeah, it's just business. Soul-crushing business if you're not strong enough to take it, shake it, then make it. And for the models who quit the biz and say, "Enough!" I say bravo for being self-aware that this sometimes painful business is not for you.

I am very happy to see that the industry is cracking down on harassment. Casting director James Scully has emerged as a powerful advocate for change, and there are wonderful former agents of mine, one being Oscar Reyes, who genuinely champion diversity and models' well-being, and this is just the beginning. There is no reason we can't give the whole industry a Tyover.

With a Tyover, I am trying to pull something unusual out of the girl and push her toward something that is marketable as a model. Truthfully, sometimes this is about just making someone a little more conventional because that's how she will get the most work as a model.

Other times—and in fact, most of the time, and the most exciting—it is not about making someone the prettiest girl in (that long-ass) line at In-N-Out Burger, but about giving her a look that is edgy, weird, interesting, or unforgettable.

There are no hard-and-fast rules for a Tyover (as in, "Tyra thinks a bob looks good on everyone! You get a bob! And YOU get a bob!"), because I am always looking at the individual girl and asking myself, "What does she need to take her look and career to the next level?" Modeling is a fluid and always-changing industry, so each model has to take trends and timing into account when she's launching her career. You don't want to go in looking like everybody else, but you also don't want to go in with a look that's so off trend you'll never get booked. (Although every blue moon, a totally out-there girl comes into the industry and rocks it from H2T—head to toe!)

Early in *Top Model*, we had a Southern stunner of a girl come on who had a very large gap between her front teeth. This was after Lauren Hutton but before Lara Stone, and I felt like it could really hurt her chances of getting booked. In person, the gap was so cute and charming, but it didn't translate on camera. I ran her photos by some agent friends of mine at different agencies, and they said they didn't think they could market her. (Yep, I get advice on Tyovers often. Off camera. Yep, TyTy gets helphelp.)

So I suggested she have a dental procedure to reduce the gap, and she was not happy with me about it. I don't blame her; I love a model who has an opinion, but I was steadfast in my belief (and advice from top agent pros) that this was something she needed to do if she seriously wanted to pursue a successful modeling career. She had a charming down South accent, all kinds of swag, the most precious full lips, cheekbones that could slice pepper jack cheese, and a Smize that could start fires. Plus, the girl could dominate a runway! As much as I admired her hustle, I did not want to see her miss out on some great opportunities because of one small trait (yeah, this is that whole difficult side of modeling I was talking about earlier). Finally, she agreed to have the dental work done.

This dynamite girl ended up winning the cycle and booking top, national modeling jobs. She still models and is an entrepreneur to boot. I scan her IG and beam with pride at how well that Southern country cutie's doing. So yeah, I was glad she took my advice. She also didn't choose to reverse the procedure, even though it wasn't permanent.

But if she wanted to open that gap today and asked me if I thought she should, I'd say yes.

But the whole situation still makes me go "Hmmmm," and I'm torn about whether I did the right thing. Closing the gap got her ready to book the most modeling jobs . . . my mission—but letting it be would have expanded the definition of beauty . . . again . . . my mission, even if it meant sacrificing lots of work. I struggle with this kind of trade-off every season of *Top Model*, in some way or another, and the dilemmas stick with me. I wear two hats: model mentor and beauty crusader. Usually they're BFFs, but sometimes they have to duke it out. So as you read this and can feel the dilemma, what would you have done? Closed the gap so she could rock more billboards and posters? Or left it alone so she could be the gap-toothed poster child? One decision is for her, the other is for, well . . . others. Maybe I should have left it alone on the show and then let her agent advise her after we wrapped. Two birds, one stone. Yeah, that's what I shoulda done. Damn. Shoulda. Woulda. Coulda. Why is everything always crystal clear years later?

CUT TO A FEW YEARS LATER, during our petite cycle (wassup my 5'7" and under cuties around the world!), I urged one of my models to take the opposite course and widen her existing gap. She went along with this suggestion, agreeing that it would help give her a certain edge. And it worked great in her photos and she rode the wave of the Lara Stone trend, the gap-toothed supermodel of that moment.

I got so much flack for this.

Flack in tweets, comments, e-mails, snail mail.

"Tyra, you minimized one girl's gap seasons ago and maximized another's. What???"

On the surface, it looks really confusing. I get it. But it's the fashion biz, so you've got to look deeper. These two beautiful girls were very different models, at very different times in an ever-changing industry. Everyone is an individual and I treat all my girls that way, by individually assessing them. There are no hard-and-fast rules as to what features work in modeling and what features don't, but there is something called a trend. Yep, the T-word again. And when a trend is coming for you, sometimes the only thing you can do is saddle up and ride it all the way to the bank. And I want as many girls as possible riding money horses of their own—a whole fleet of flawsome cowgirls—so when I see something that may stand in the way of a girl (and her bank account) reaching her full potential, that's when the extra nuances of a Tyover come in. And yep, the whole tug-of-war starts up all over again. Should I? Shouldn't I?

It takes a certain look and spirit to get in the door of the modeling world, but even once you're in, the client and the industry are still going to have a lot to say. A whole helluva lot. Every time a model gets hired, she may wanna walk on set and say, "Take me as I am." But get this: The very core of the modeling powers that be is not to just take you as you are. They may fall in love with some of your flawsome features (heck yeah!), but often they take you and make you and bake you into whatever different version of you works best for their brand/magazine/product/agency/idea.

It's also business, and they take care of theirs just as much as you have to take care of yours. You can always say no, and you should if you feel like something you are being asked to do will compromise your health, safety, reputation, or standards. Shoot, a big "Hell to the no!" would be quite appropriate. When the high-fashion world was asking me to lose a lot of weight, my mother and I decided to walk away because we knew I'd be jeopardizing my mental and physical well-being if I did so. (I mean, have you picked up on how much I like food by how much I talk about it in this book?) Refusing to lose weight was a calculated risk that I took, and it paid off.

However, if you are a model who is just getting started, and you cry and run off set the first time someone suggests you dye your hair, you are also taking a risk—one that might not pay off. You're playing it too safe, boo. C'mon, be open. *Hair grows back!*

Don't love your tresses transformation? Cover it up. Lace front wigs are one of the world's greatest inventions, right up there with talk-to-text and single-serving packets of barbecue sauce. So wear 'em! Shoot, I got tons of wigs in every color and texture in storage. Hit me up if you're willing to dig through the piles to find one that suits your fancy.

Alert, alert! Yeah, this is just a photo of Mama and me at a banquet, but check out my natural hair!

Carolyn: One of Tyra's biggest talents with makeovers is that she helps you to think outside the box. Sometimes that takes a nudge, sometimes it takes a shove, but once you're outside that box, you can't believe you wasted so much time in there. And I speak from experience here—I've gotten a Tyover myself!

A few years ago, I was getting ready for a black-tie event. I'd always interpreted black tie pretty literally—I wore all black. It was conservative, safe, and, I have to admit, a little boring. Especially because I paired it with the pageboy hairdo and makeup that I wore every day to the office. No frills, no shine, no fun.

Tyra threw that right back in the closet.

She got me a floor-length purple and blue gown with a patterned hem and rhinestone details around the neck. It was a mix of an exotic caftan and a beautiful Indian sari. I never would have picked out something that colorful and sparkly for myself, but I looked like a queen! She styled my hair in full-bodied, shoulder-grazing curls with a dramatic smoky eye and lip gloss that shone as bright as a diamond.

When I arrived at the event, I got compliments like you wouldn't believe! A couple of people didn't even recognize me. And boo, I even got hit on a couple of times!

So thanks, baby girl, for giving Mama a night to remember!

Tyra: Now, I didn't give Mama a makeover that time because she looked bad before. No—she looked fine; she looked good! But that was one of those times where fine and good didn't cut it. I wanted her to know what it felt like to look stunning!

But still, that was more of a traditional makeover, and not like the Tyovers I give on *Top Model.* A Tyover is about fashion and modeling, whereas a traditional makeover is about making you the prettiest version of yourself. In the modeling world, the prettiest version of you sometimes translates to "boring and commercial," and that won't necessarily get you booked in Paris or Milan. Girls sometimes hate the results of their Tyovers because they just want to look like the prettiest girl in the club (sometimes a Tyover even takes more than one try to get it right, because a hairdresser has a different vision than I do), whereas I'm often trying to make them look like a strange, elegant, eccentric piece of art that stands out on the runway. Sometimes that takes a bowl cut, and let's face it, no girl wants a bowl cut because most boys bouncing to EDM aren't tryna holler at a girl with Paul McCartney's do.

So, let's be clear—just like being an amazing home cook who

I would always do crazy makeup at home and get Mama to take Polaroids. I still do makeup like this on my *Top Model* hopefuls all the time!

hosts the best Thanksgiving and being the head chef at a five-star restaurant require separate skill sets, being a pretty girl and being a model are also two different things. Models are not always pretty, but they have a look that translates an idea and that can be sold. They can be odd, quirky, weird, awkward, debatable beauties. I gotta admit, those ones are my faves. I wish I could take credit for this next quote, but it was actually my friend who's also a former model, Yaniece, who said, "You can't be a high-fashion model unless you cried your way through adolescence." There are beautiful, gorgeous girls everywhere on this globe who smoke models on the beauty front hands down. I see them every day. Whew, child, they are *stunners*! But not necessarily models.

Carolyn: Lord, is that true. Sometimes, if I close my eyes, I can still hear Tyra's boo-hoos echoing down our hallway. I wish I coulda wiped that pain away by telling her what was coming, but she never would have believed me anyway!

Tyra: Like I said, high-fashion models often tend to have something a little odd or weird about them. Their eyes might be too close together, too far apart, their forehead is probably too big, their chin is probably too short, their lips are probably too wide or too narrow or too small or too big . . . all the things that people give you so much crap for in elementary, junior high, and high school. If you were that popular cheerleader and everybody on campus (boys and girls) wanted to take you to prom—girl, you didn't cry enough. High fashion is probably not for you. And that's OK.

On *Top Model*, when all my girls are crying about being teased when they were little because they were so awkward, I'm like "Mmm-hmm, high fashion. Let me just open these editorial velvet ropes for you, child. Come right on in."

When you see the girls on *Top Model*, it's not just a coincidence that there are all types of different looks up there. I deliberately choose to aggressively expand the definition of beauty so that throughout the various seasons, everyone watching can find someone who kinda looks like them. That way, when I'm showering these atypical model hopefuls on TV with all kinds of kudos about how fierce their pics are and how stunning they are, young viewers at home who share some of those attributes can begin to accept what makes them different and unique.

That is, in a nutshell, what I want to do with *Top Model*: expand the definition of beauty so that women can learn to appreciate themselves, and also give them a whole toolbox full of tricks to fix or flaunt what they've got.

Let's face it: A lot of women want to look like everybody else—because their entire life, they've been told that's what beauty is. They want to be cookie-cutter pretty, but I ain't about using cookie cutters. I'm trying to hand-shape each cookie into something special. It might be lumpy and bumpy and no one at Starbucks wants to buy it, but it'll make the whole darn world a lot tastier. And it'll take fashion's breath away, too.

And maybe the boys standing in that long-ass In-N-Out Burger line, too, one day.

OUT OF YOUR COMFORT ZONE VS. THE NO-GO ZONE

When you step Out of Your Comfort Zone, it is important to stop stepping before you get into the Uncomfy Zone. Out of Your Comfort Zone feels new and exciting, and you're discovering aspects of yourself you never knew existed.

The No-Go Zone is where you do things that make you feel worse (not better) about yourself, and where you make choices you might regret.

Avoid the No-Go Zone at all costs.

OUT OF YOUR COMFORT ZONE

- New hair color
- New haircut
- Shaving your head
- Skipping armpit shaving
- Going natural
- Adding hair extensions for the first time
- Overcoming fears (like posing with spiders)
- Taking risks (like floating in a wind tunnel)
- Dressing in drag

THE NO-GO ZONE

➤ Hanging out solo, in a nonwork environment,
with any men (or women) you do not trust

➤ Stealing from the company you work for, helping
a coworker cheat, or falsifying information

➤ Anyone, anywhere, ever who offers you work in
return for sexual favors

➤ Drugs (including alcohol) and anyone who
pressures you to do them

➤ Crazy weight-loss tips or starvation diets

➤ Signing contracts you have not read or do not
have the opportunity to have a lawyer review.
Anyone who throws a fit about you wanting to
understand something before you sign it does not
have your best interests in mind.

Carolyn: I'm always touched when I hear Tyra rally for all the atypical girls who break the mold, 'cause I was one of those girls, and I know Tyra was, too. She may be fierce and flawsome (and damn near six feet tall) today, but I know there's still a skinny, insecure eleven-year-old girl hidden deep inside under all those wigs and false lashes. The cookie-cutter girls . . . hmmmm . . . they're too worried about being perfect to have much flavor. It's the girls like us—the imperfect ones—who spice it up (and have all the good dance moves, too).

Tyra: It's easy to define *cookie-cutter.* You hear those words and an image probably pops into your head immediately. You know exactly what I'm talking about—that person with features that are really pretty but also really common. Lips just so, hair like, y'know . . . that. Nothing that really stands out. But wait a sec. Think about *different.* How can you even begin to define *different*? You've got to think about that one for a minute. Chew on it and flip it upside down and backward in your mind.

There's so much to different! It could be mismatched-colored eyes, freckles, a crooked smile, one dimple, a birthmark, a shaved head. . . . Different is infinite. You never know what to expect, and that, to me, is so exciting.

My pet peeve is when we give a girl an amazing Tyover and she does really well on *Top Model,* then as soon as the show is over, she goes back to her normal hair and has no career ('cause her boyfriend didn't like her pixie cut, or some nonsense like that). I'm like, "Girl, hello?"

I'm not saying you have to choose between having a man and being different. No, not at all. I'm just saying get you a man (or a woman) who appreciates different. Those are the good ones, anyway. I had one who loved and was attracted to me no matter—a weave, a slick-back, cornrows, my natural no-relaxer-textured hair, and even me with my scarf tied on my head in the morning. And he hated when I wore bangs.

Dang, maybe I shoulda kept him.

GO WITH OPTION C

Tyra: I have two selves. I have Tyra, and I have the Thing.

Tyra puts her son to bed each night with a sloppy kiss, loves frozen dinners, holds business meetings in clothes she's worn two days in a row, calls her mama too much, and sits on the couch in sweatpants sending e-mails while licking the frozen dinner paper container because the sauce is just too good to waste (I mean, have you had that Indian food from Amy's?).

The Thing hosts all those shows with *America* in the title, was in all those magazines, and yeah, the Thing is a supermodel.

Another supermodel, Cindy Crawford (my idol—*aughhhhhhhh!* I love that woman!), introduced me to the Thing—that was what she called herself after she'd gone through the works. You get the full face of makeup, you get the hair extensions, and then a few more hair extensions, the body makeup, the boob tape and push-up bra, the soft ambient lighting, the photographer who knows your good side, a retoucher who says, "Poof, it's gone," to any cellulite, stretch marks, zits, wrinkles, bruises (those damn pointy doorknobs in my house!), and a whole team of people (and their assistants) whose sole purpose for the next three hours is to make sure you don't have visible panty lines, a double chin, or kale in your teeth.

Carolyn: But damn, sometimes I have to look twice before it sinks in that the Thing came out of me all those years ago.

Tyra: The Thing looks so damn good because it is the Thing's job to look so damn good. There are a lot of people paid a lot of money surrounding the Thing to make sure that happens. As a model, the Thing is your product. It is the commodity that you sell, but it is not who you *are*.

Mama never let me forget that.

🫦 *Carolyn:* "When they say they don't want you for a job, they're not talking about you. The Tyra Banks they know . . . she is not you," I'd say. "She is a product on the shelf. The Thing. But you, my dear—you are my TyTy. And you will forever be my special little girl. Never forget it."

Sometimes, I would grab and shake Tyra. I would have hit her over the head (only with something soft, like a pillow or a bag of popcorn) if that was what it took to drill it in. I did not want her to let these powerful bosses in black get to her, because I knew that if she stayed focused, one day they would look at her in awe.

👁️ 👁️ *Tyra:* Being a model gave me a behind-the-scenes, up-close-and-all-up-in-it relationship with beauty transformation, because I saw just how much pulling and tugging went into making the Thing come to life. Most women don't get to see that. Don't get it twisted—many beauty tutorials today have filters, editing, and feels-real-but-ain't tricks. So many people see a produced, finished version of the Thing, and if they're at all insecure (aren't we all, to some extent?), they end up comparing themselves to it. Damn you, Thing! So I say to you—yeah, the You who is reading this right now . . .

Stop. Do not do that!

But still, I don't blame ya if you do, because sometimes it

doesn't seem like you have that many options when it comes to how you look. In fact, it usually seems like you have two: option A and option B.

Option A is to be completely natural, standing there in nothing but a pair of granny panties without even a touch of mascara, no retouching, and bad posture. Some women who see that start sweatin' in their Spanx and doubting, thinking maybe they're just fake, superficial chicks after all.

Option B is the red carpet and the glossy spreads of fashion magazines, full of women who are 5'10", 110 pounds (tops); and social media, where some stars of the 'gram are edited until they're just one blur away from turning into an anime character. The message of this option is "Screw anything and everything that's not perfect, so you better start starvin' and sculptin' now cuz I look like this IRL, bitches!"

I'm here to advocate for option C: You do you.

I love me some makeup because I believe it is the great beauty equalizer. It's leveling the playing field one cosmetics bag at a time.

Want cheekbones? Honey, paint 'em on!

Want fierce brows? A little pencil here, a little brow groomer there, and boom! You just framed your Smize like it's hanging in the Metropolitan Museum of Art!

Need a little look-at-me boost before you walk into a room? Gimme an *L*, gimme an *I*, gimme a *P*, gimme an *S*, gimme a *T*, gimme an *I* . . .

Wait, that's got too many letters in it! You got it—you know I'm spelling out *lipstick*. I can move on. OK. OK . . .

As much as I want to tell women to be confident in who they are, I also want them to know there's no shame in a little contour here and a little tuck there. Stand there in those granny panties, but let me add an hour of makeup to you, a wig, and a wind machine, and a retouch blur or two because you deserve to feel just as glamorous as all those Photoshopped skinny chicks (and curvy ones, too).

Every woman deserves to feel beautiful, and I love, love, love being able to show a woman how little it takes to show off a new side of herself. When people come up to me on the street or at events and want to take a selfie, I don't just snap the photo and get out of there—I'm tryna get them the best damn selfie they've ever taken in their lives. "Here, add a little lip gloss, and we're gonna put some on your cheekbones, too. Flip all of your hair over to the side like that and elongate your neck. Tilt your head this way and put your chin down just a bit. Now lemme just move this candle over here so your good side is lit. . . ." And snap.

I don't need my *Top Model* wind machine and a whole team. I just need a camera phone and whatever prop I've got on hand. Then I show her the picture on her own phone, and her face transforms into shock, disbelief, and Oh-my-God-Tyra-I-can't-believe-this-is-me joy. This mom/waitress/daughter/bus driver/DMV worker/dentist/accountant/marketing exec/kindergarten teacher who swears she doesn't care about makeup and has never been photogenic is smiling so hard she starts to get a headache at how good she is looking. To me, that elation is the money spot. It makes me so happy. That's what I think the Tyra personal brand (Lordy, I am up here talking in the third person. Forgive me!) is all about: You don't have to chase something that's impossible and live up to some BS, but you can dream and have fun and enhance what you have. Beauty is not a limited quantity that only gets doled out to a few. Beauty is not one of those tiny appetizers with three bites of hamachi—it's family-style fried chicken. There's plenty to go around, so everyone should dig in and take however much they want.

I can't stress that enough, whether you work on a photo set, set the record straight in courtrooms, or work any other job between, you have to follow your gut (even if it's sucked in) and do what makes you comfortable. Maybe that's a lot, maybe it's a little, maybe it's none at all.

It is about you.

End of story.

So when you feel forced to choose between A and B, just C your way out of it.

Carolyn: You just need to read the title of this book to know how I feel about cookie-cutter. It's predictable, obvious, boring. And yeah, cookie-cutter girls often get preferential treatment in life. It's OK, though. Why? Because they also tend to peak early. So, if you've always been a cookie-cutter dame and are now eighteen years old, enjoy that beauty while it lasts. 'Cause once twenty-eight comes around the bend, you may need to throw a beauty going-away party. I'll attend. Especially if you've got ice cream. Make mine chocolate chip.

The late bloomers, those awkward girls who cry themselves through adolescence, they are the ones who need encouragement and hugs. They have struggled, cried themselves to sleep night after night. And now, it's their turn. There were no pretty-girl handouts for them, so when that pretty bus stops and invites them on, they are a bit confused and have to be convinced they can step aboard.

After years of crying herself to sleep over her reflection, when that bus stopped for Tyra, she hopped on. But before she took her front-row seat, she held that door open for millions of other girls to get on the bus. She's still holding it. I bet her arms hurt.

But it's worth it.

EMBRACE YOUR BOOTY

Tyra: Everyone thought I was on vacation, just letting it all hang out. But really, I was in Australia shooting for *Top Model* when those photos were taken. People think I got caught during some me time, but child, I was posing. For you.

Anyway, you might know the photos I'm talking about. Me. In a brown strapless one-piece swimsuit, on the beach, my hair's flowing and my ass and thighs, well . . . some say those are ummm . . . overflowing. I call it curvy, thick, sexy, voluptuous. But the world called it something else.

Fat.

During that photo shoot, we knew that there were paparazzi in the distance. My security was trained to recognize the glare on a lens, no matter how far away, and when they saw that signature reflection of light way up in the trees, we knew exactly what it was.

Whatever, we shrugged it off. Paparazzi come with the territory of being in the public eye, especially on a beach. A beach complete with a crew of about fifteen people doing a photo shoot. That #squad ain't blendin' in. We were some busy people, too. We had eight more shoots and locations to go to in Sydney that day, so we couldn't waste time chasing the "paps" off every time one popped up.

After my last shot on the beach, as I was walking back to the location van, a paparazzo had emerged from the bushes and was right in the sand. I said hello, joked and asked him if he got the shot, and I was on my way. I didn't get annoyed until he showed up at lunch miles away from the beach. "Oh, come on," I thought. "Can't this dude go bother somebody else? There has got to be some famous Australian around here somewhere. Where the heck is Nicole Kidman when you need her?"

I dropped some hints to him that he should be done, and he picked up on none of them—not even the one where I straight-up— yet politely—asked him to leave us alone so we could eat our juicy Australian steaks in peace.

He snapped away through the appetizer, main course, and dessert. So, my team and I brainstormed ways that we could have a little fun with him. As soon as we'd paid the check, we put our plan into action. Everyone at our table pulled out their camera phones and we chased him down the sidewalk, snapping away. We wanted him to see how it felt.

We were lighthearted, smiling and laughing the whole time, and the "photo shoot" lasted all of fifteen feet. But someone wasn't smiling at all. My pap was pissed.

"Come on, dude." I said. "It's all love. We were just having a little fun being you." Then I got in the van, and we drove away and had forgotten all about it as we continued to shoot around the city. When I laid my head on my pillow that night at the hotel, I'd forgotten it all.

Two weeks later, I landed at LAX airport and was back in the U.S. of A. I enjoyed Australia but it felt good to be home. As soon as the plane touched down, my cell phone was blowing up. Countless texts and voice mails, asking me if I was OK. Was I OK? Of course I was OK. I'd just spent three weeks shooting *Top Model* and had crowned a cha-cha diva winner who was gonna win the hearts of America and the world.

But then more messages started to flood in. Messages that revealed what the "Are you OK" concerned ones were all about: me on the cover of every tabloid out there, with headlines like **AMERICA'S NEXT TOP WADDLE** and **THIGH-RA BANKS** and **TYRA TOPS 200 LBS!!!** I about died when I saw that—of laughter. I thought it was crazy, but I did not take it seriously. But I did recognize that the people who sent them to me seemed to be enjoying every minute of it.

You don't need me to tell you this, because anyone who's ever accidentally opened their photo to the selfie cam when they weren't expecting it knows—pictures can tell all kinds of cray stories. Oh yes, I was bigger than usual at the time, but it was nothing that was outside my normal "bigger phase" range.

The photos had just come out and people were coming up to me like, "Oh my God, you look great! How did you lose all that weight in a week?" If they didn't know that it was damn near impossible for someone to lose forty pounds in seven days, I didn't consider it my job to enlighten them. I didn't tell people that I hadn't lost any weight at all, that it was all in the difference a paparazzi photo can make. I just tried to brush it off and change the subject. "Oh, well, I don't know . . . but damn, girl, *you* look fantastic! What type of weave hair are you using these days?"

Cut to a day later. I was standing in line at the grocery store. (Yes, I shop for my own groceries often.) The woman in front of me was looking at the tabloid magazine covers, then turned around and looked me straight in the eyes. There was no "OMG, Tyra, I can't believe you do your own grocery shopping!" look on her face. Instead she said, "If they're calling *you* fat, what am I?" And she said it through tears.

That was when it hit me—this whole incident wasn't funny, and it wasn't just about me.

No pun intended, but it was bigger than me. Much bigger.

I called my *Tyra Banks Show* producers from the car on the way home. We worked on producing the response-to-the-tabloids show for about a week, and I had intense sessions with my team of producers to bounce ideas off them and figure out exactly what I wanted to say. (Thanks, Lauren Berry-Blincoe and John Redmann!) At first, I was going to end my diatribe by saying, "To everyone who goes around calling me and other women fat, f*ck you!" and flip off the camera. When the show aired, we'd just bleep out my words and blur my hands.

Then we sat back and realized that we wanted this moment to be more poignant than cursing, and we didn't want to bleep or blur any part of it out, so we rewrote it. I tried so many different versions, like "Forget you!" or "Kiss my butt," and even called the Standards and Practices, the censor police of network television. "Can I say 'ass' on TV?" I asked.

We had a winner.

The day of shooting, I was dressed in my little talk show dress, looking prim and proper. But something felt off. I called out to my stylist, Yaniece, "Do you still have that swimsuit from Australia?"

"The swimsuit?" she asked.

"Yeah, *the* swimsuit."

"Girl, yeah. It's with all that *Top Model* stuff over there in that suitcase."

"Get it out," I said.

"Why?"

I started taking off my clothes.

"What are you doing?" she asked, looking at me like I was crazier than I already was.

"Just help me put it on," I said.

She helped me yank it up, and I was about ready to exit my dressing room when I thought, "Oh shoot, I may be brave, but I ain't stupid." I called over Valente, my longtime makeup artist, who was also on the Australian beach with me, to put some body makeup on my legs, and run some Victoria's Secret–like shimmer down the front of my thighs (a trick that makes it look like there's a muscle there when there ain't).

Then I walked out the door, straight to the stage.

When I entered that set in *that* swimsuit and nothing else, my staff and many of my producers were as shocked as the studio audience.

Carolyn: I was sitting in my living room in front of the TV, sipping on my daily can of ginger ale, when Tyra strutted onto the set of her talk show sporting the same bathing suit that was plastered on the cover of every gossip magazine around the world.

Of course, she had told me that she was going to address the paparazzi's blatant attempt at public humiliation, but not dressed like that! With every sip, I grew more and more proud.

Tyra: I addressed the audience and was as real and as raw as was humanly possible, and ended it yelling, "Kiss my FAT ass!" Oh, I slapped my own ass super hard when I said "fat," too. I had wanted the whole speech to be strong, empowering, *fierce*. But now, as the audience screamed and cheered and teared up and even sobbed, I realized I was crying, too. What the hell? I was just laughing about all of this a week ago. But now, I was feeling weak and vulnerable. *WTF?*

I needed to be strong. I needed to be a warrior. I needed to be an example to women everywhere that they could survive this body shaming without letting it break them down. I ran straight to the control booth to my director, Brian.

"Brian," I said, wiping snot from my nose, "I started to cry out there. So we gotta do it again. And I want you to end the 'Kiss my fat ass' part with a shot close on my face—strong and defiant. There was this woman in the grocery store, and I can't have her see me all teary. Nobody should see me crying. It's weak."

Brian looked at me—actually, he looked *through* me—then started walking around the booth, turning off each and every monitor. When he was done, he turned to me and said, "Tyra, go home."

"What?" I said.

"Go home," he repeated. "Yes, you cried. Yes, you were vulnerable. But it was real. It was you. And I'm not gonna say it again after this. Go. Home."

So, I did as he said. I went home. I hardly slept for the next two weeks, until it aired.

And the day it aired changed my life forever.

Carolyn: "Kiss my fat ass!" Whew! Those four words that Tyra said—no, *yelled*—were not what I had expected. But I was overjoyed! By the time she slapped her butt, I had leapt off the couch, spilled ginger ale on my shirt, and had tears rolling down my cheeks. Tyra spoke in defense of all of us who have witnessed or experienced the physical and emotional chains that are forced upon women throughout our lives. It was as if she was screaming in unison with all of our voices: "Enough is friggin' enough!" The resounding response from women and girls around the planet said it all. We were tired of feeling that we are worth nothing more than what we weigh.

Tyra: That butt slap was felt everywhere—from beauty salons to office buildings to locker rooms to school playgrounds to damn near every news and online outlet in the darn universe. I saw the gorgeous and talented Adele at an Alicia Keys event and she wrapped her arms around me and thanked me from her beautiful body and soul profusely. Women (and men, too) from all over the world were writing in about how much what I said meant to them. A week later at intermission of the musical *Rent* in NYC, a woman pulled me aside and said the moment saved her life, that she had a handful of pills but experienced that moment and immediately called a suicide hotline that ended up saving her life. *Time* magazine named me one of the most influential people of the year next to Barack Obama, Oprah Winfrey, and Richard Branson (and in the Heroes and Pioneers category, no less). And the speech made it onto *TV Guide Magazine*'s 60 Greatest Talk Show Moments list.

I had no idea it would lead to all of that. But I realized it had this impact because it was a real moment. At the time I taped it, I thought real meant polished. A do-over. Perfection. But if I had delivered that speech how I wanted to—cool and calculated, and yeah, 100 percent "strong," like I wasn't bothered one bit by people calling me fat—it would not have resonated the powerful way it did.

I believe in those words that I said on my talk show just as much today as I did when I first said them, more than ten years ago. And just in case you weren't there back then to experience the moment, and even if you were, I've brought it here . . . to you:

I love my mama. She has helped me to be a strong woman so I can overcome these kind of attacks, but if I had lower self-esteem, I would probably be starving myself right now. But, that's exactly what is happening to other women all over this country. So, I have something to say to all of you that have something nasty to say about me or other women who are built like me . . . women whose names you know, women whose names you don't, women who've been picked on, women whose husbands put them down, women at work or girls in school—I have one thing to say to you: Kiss my fat ass!

Carolyn: This epic moment was a culmination of all that I had worked so hard to instill in Tyra. She had sprouted her own wings and was flying high.

Fat ass and all.

5 ASS-ENTIAL TYRA TIPS FOR BETTER BODY IMAGE

1. Make a list of what you love about your body. Add something new every month.

Sit down and take the time to do this. Get a pen and paper, and set a timer for five minutes. Write down as many things as you can think of that you like about yourself, and it is OK if it is just one, then post that list someplace you'll see it every day (like on the bathroom mirror). Once a month, revisit the list and add something new.

2. Self-care, boo!

Get your nails did, get your hair did, take a bubble bath, take a long nap, eat a cupcake, binge a season of of *Big Little Lies* (or *Top Model*, just sayin'), read an entire book in one sitting, spend some time alone. Whatever it is that makes you feel good and rested, carve out the time to do it.

3. Fake it till you make it.

Pretend you're confident and love your body. Next time you're at the pool, stroll around without a cover-up instead of hiding behind a towel. Do all the things you think a body-confident woman would do, and you might start believing yourself.

4. **Stop talking ish about other women.**
If you find yourself wanting to criticize the way someone else looks, just stop. Change the subject. Or even
better, say something nice.

5. **Ditch the triggers.**
Try to cut out the things and people that make you
feel bad. If you have a 105-pound friend who's always
talking about how she could lose a few, take a break.
Maybe she's not your best going-out-to-dinner buddy. If
Instagram makes you feel sad, stop the scroll.

CHOOSE HEALTHY OVER SKINNY

Tyra: My weight is like Cardi B's beautiful
booty while she's twerking: It goes up and it goes down and then
back up and then back down—over and over again. And to be
honest, my mood is happiest when I'm up. I know right now
you're like, "*What?*" But let me explain. I'm happiest bigger because I'm not restricting myself at all. For me, food is pleasure,
pleasure, pleasure. I don't drink, I don't smoke, and have never
done drugs, so food is my vice. When I'm thick, you better damn
well believe that I am celebrating like it's my birthday at every
damn meal.

Carolyn: Tyra and I are both ice cream addicts. No matter what city or country we are in, we will find the top ice cream parlor. In New York, we used to go to the bodega and get about eight different kinds, then take those bad boys back to her condo. We wouldn't even put them in a bowl; we'd just line them all up on the sink like piano keys, get a spoon, and travel the counter of pints. We've had some of our best business ideas playing ice cream keyboards! I think the idea for her to do her own swimsuit calendar and to do two versions, an edgy one and a commercial one, came from those "ice cream musical" sessions.

I'm lactose intolerant now, so I know if I eat ice cream I'll have an upset stomach and be running to the powder room all night. But sh*t, I eat it anyway. Pun intended.

Tyra: When I was growing up, we'd go to the Häagen-Dazs shop on Hollywood Boulevard every weekend. I will eat almost any ice cream flavor, as long as there's no chocolate in it. (Yeah, I'm the fool who doesn't like chocolate, but I ain't mad at cookies 'n' cream.) Just give it to me, baby. And I like my cream straight up. No cone.

For the specialty, boutique places, like Salt & Straw, McConnell's, and Jeni's, I will stand in line and wait and wait. I don't care if there are thirty people in front of me—I'll stand there all anxious like I'm there waiting for the Black Friday sale to drop. When I was at my biggest, I would get dessert (usually ice cream) after lunch and dinner. And, like I said, I felt great.

But now, as I write this, I've dropped a few pounds. Why? I've got this old ankle injury that keeps recurring, and the last time I twisted it was on the set of Drake's "Childs Play" video. "Oh,

Tyra, you gotta see the instant replay of your cheesecake-smush-face moment!" said one of Drake's boys to me. I ran to the monitor before they were about to turn it off and *twist*, it happened again. And I woke up the next morn with more pain than ever before. If you caught me running onto the *America's Got Talent* stage to give an impromptu makeover on my debut episode in unsexy white sneakers, blame the ankle (but don't blame sexy Aubrey "Drake" Graham; ain't his fault). My doctor said if I drop some weight, along with doing rigorous physical therapy, my ankle will heal faster, better, stronger. So, I've been going to cycling classes, balancing in yoga classes, doing Pilates, and yeah, eating healthier. I'm more energetic and my ankle is soooo much healthier. And yeah, that feels good, too.

Sometimes my mom and I get into it over healthy eating. She eats any- and everything she wants. She's a cheeseburger, fries, and shake three times a week kind of eater, whereas I'm now more of the burger and no bun kind of girl.

But dammit, I want my momma to be healthy! I had my son when I was older, and I want her to be around to watch him grow up because York is *obsessed* with his nana. We were FaceTiming with York recently, and she told me she'd had pancakes and bacon for breakfast. Again.

"Choose life, not bacon slice!" I yelled.

"Oh, pshaw," she responded. "Bacon ain't killed nobody but the pig."

"Bacon nobahbee PIG!" repeated Grandma's number one fan, a.k.a. York.

I respect my mama more than anyone, but she knows that ain't true. And now I gotta unteach my lil pumpkin this at the same time I'm trying to get him to think lima beans and rutabaga are the most delicious things on the planet so that I can airplane another spoonful into his mouth for dinner.

Carolyn: After my early teen years, I had a slim, tight waistline, but now I have all these bloops, one muffin top on top of another on top of another. Tyra's always trying to help pull my shirt out of waist creases because it gets stuck in the dents. So one day I said, "Well, let me show you something I can do that none of you can!"

I held my arms up, started leaning side to side, and did a whole routine with accordion sounds coming out of my mouth.

"I cannot believe you are playing your body, Mama," Tyra said.

"Every negative you can turn into a positive," I said, and just kept right on playing my body accordion.

You got some rolls round your middle? Show your hidden talents and strike up a tune for the kiddies; they'll love it.

Tyra: Remember when I told you my mama is crazy? The body accordion just backs me up. Ma is disgusted (or at least pretends to be) by anything that is healthy. I mentioned the need for her to drink more water last year, and you know what she said?

"Water? Ugh."

What?

But honestly, I get it. A lot of it is a generational thing. Twenty years from now, York will probably come to me saying, "Mom, why are you eating that quinoa and that kale? That's disgusting! Don't you know that can kill you? You need to make your salad with these fermented, oxygenated bubble-gut greens that come from the droppings of a Himalayan mountain goat."

And I'll look at him and go, "Get the hell out of my face, boy. Kale ain't killed nobody but the leaf."

But the difference with me is I'll probably eat the goat poop.

Carolyn: Goodness gracious, I just read this chapter and I sound insane in the membrane. I love all my grand-babies and wanna live to see my newest one give his mama hell like she gave me. So maybe I'll trade in this slice of streaky, fatty bacon for the healthier Canadian kind, and these buttermilk pancakes with extra syrup can be swapped for some naturally sweet Scandinavian crackers. Does it taste as good? Almost. But is it time for a change? Hell to the yes! So thank you, TyTy, for mothering your mama and introducing me to healthy choices that tickle my taste buds, and for making me see the skim/low-cal/lite light. But two liters of water a day? Lord, help me.

NON-SKINNY PEOPLE WHO I THINK ARE SEXY AS HELL

I like a bit of booty on my models, my missies, my matrons, and my men. I think these people are some fine-ass human beings.

- **ASHLEY GRAHAM**: This statuesque supermodel stunner is also my new *America's Next Top Model* judge and my girl! She's the queen of the Curve-a-listas!

- **ZACH MIKO**: The first supermodel to come out of Brawn, IMG's plus-size male model division. Chiseled, chunky, and oh so funky (and oh so fine as hell!).

- **CHRISTINA HENDRICKS**: A redhead with curves so hot they could start fires.

- **KATE UPTON**: My *Sports Illustrated* cover girl sister from another mister.

- **VINCE VAUGHN**: 6'5" and looking good, boo. No beanpoles here.

- **AMBER ROSE**: A beauty and a booty on a mission to stop slut shaming. I can definitely get behind that behind.

➤ **DASCHA POLANCO**: Orange is the new black, and bootyful is the new beautiful.

➤ The bearded man in the plaid shirt sitting next to me at this Malibu café right now as I type. (Damn, your thick lumbersexual ass is fine, boo!)

10

LEARN SOMETHING FROM THIS!

Carolyn: You can't protect your children from everything. You've got to let them bump into walls sometimes, because that's the only way they're gonna learn.

So when Tyra came to me and said she was going to add singing to her body of talents, I had instant visions of her smashing into a concrete wall like one of those crash-test dummies!

Tyra: It wasn't because I wanted to sing that I decided I wanted to be a singer. I wanted to make music videos and perform live, get the crowd on their feet and have them yelling and losing their mind. J.Lo was doing it and killin' it big-time, and she didn't start her career as a singer, so why couldn't I?

And yeah, I know what you're thinking. "Tyra, why you think you can sing when you never sang before?"

Well, I had experience. My rap name was Ty Loc Ski Mac Dog, and I even wrote my own rap (which I still know today and plan to perform at York's eighteenth birthday party). It went a little something like this:

"I'm 34A, but that's okay, cuz the rest of my body is just touché.
I'm five foot nine. I look so fine. Yes, all my fellas are so divine.

When I'm finished with this, you might as well just dismiss
All the other female rappers, cuz y'all just piss.
My eyes so green. They look so keen.
If you had one look, you know what I mean.
My hair's so brown, it is always down,
And on my face, there never is a frown.
When you and I meet, you will not stand.
So get on your knees, and kiss Ty's hand.
Go Tyra, get busy, go Tyra . . ."

Oh yeah, that was ninth grade. And I just wrote that rap because I was lost in algebra and took a lil break from trying to figure out what x is when $5(-3x - 2) - (x - 3) = -4(4x + 5) + 13$.

Hmmm, yeah, I probably should have stopped right there.

Carolyn: Tyra could carry a tune; I had to give her that. She could also dance really well, even though she wasn't Janet Jackson. But I knew that if she wanted to be a singer, she was going to have to be a damn good singer because she wasn't going to be able to sneak in the back door. No, if Miss Tyra Banks, Supermodel, decided to sing, the spotlight was going to be on her from that first note, and if she sounded more like a screech owl than a songbird, she was never going to live it down.

I was on pins and needles from that first time she mentioned singing, but I always told my children that I would support them no matter what they decided to do—even if what I thought they decided to do was a . . . ummm . . . s t r e t c h.

When Tyra came to me and said she was setting up meetings with music producers, all I did was nod.

"Mm-hmm," I said. "Have they heard ya sing?"
They had not.

👁 👁 *Tyra:* When I decide something, I go hard. I don't just dip in a pedicured pinky; I belly flop. I have tunnel vision, and from the moment I decided I was going to be a singer, it became my obsession. You can do anything if you put your mind to it, right? Well, maybe . . .

I got a leading vocal coach and started taking lessons with him three times a week. Ashlee Simpson had the time slot right before me, so I could hear her finishing up when I arrived. She sounded good. I'd sit there, listening to her with sweat dripping in my armpits. I knew I didn't sound half as good as she did, but still, when her time was up and I was on, Ashlee and I would exchange pleasantries in the waiting room, then I'd go in there and not-so-pleasantly sing my ass off for my coach.

Nothing about it felt natural, and it wasn't fun. I was stretching and straining, trying to hit notes like my life depended on it. When I'd leave, I'd think, "You know, this whole being a singer thing would work out so great if I just didn't . . . have to sing." I wanted that Milli Vanilli kinda career. Really, was lip-synching to someone else's voice so bad?

As soon as word got out that I was considering embarking on a music career, I had some of the best producers and songwriters in the world agreeing to work with me. My access to top-level talent was astounding. Was it because I had the voice of an angel? Hell no. It was because I was a Victoria's Secret Angel. When they heard me sing, they weren't hearing notes. Perhaps they were hearing potential banknotes.

I had been nominated for a Teen Choice Award that year for

best model, and while I was sitting in the audience, I got to talking with Kobe Bryant, who was sitting in the row behind me.
"What you doing this summer?" he asked me.

"Oh, nothing," I said. "Just traveling a ton for modeling. What
about you?"

"I'm cutting an album."

I about jumped out my damn awards show chair. "Get me on
it!" I said. "Let me sing on it! I can sing, and I'll even do it for
free!"

"For free?" he said.

"Oh yeah, for free, for free!"

Cut to a few days later, and I'm all up in the studio singing the
hook on Kobe's first single, which is called "K.O.B.E." My chorus
goes a little something like this: "K-O-B-E I L-O-V-E you, and I
think you are very fine. If you give me one chance, I promise to
love you. And be with you forever more." His A&R guy was freaking out about how good it was. We had a hit on our hands!

The single turned into more than I imagined. We even shot a
fancy music video with superdirector Hype Williams and were
scheduled to perform the song live at the NBA All-Star Weekend. I wore this little H2T denim outfit, and I sang my heart out,
telling K.O.B.E. how much I L-O-V-Ed him, but I could feel myself getting more and more nervous as the song went on. This
was my chance to show the world I could sing, but the camera
was barely on me. Whenever it would turn my way, it just stayed
on me for a few seconds. "What the hell?" I thought. "Am I blowing it?"

At the end of the performance, I found out why. It wasn't my
singing that the camera hated. It was the busted zipper on my
Canadian tuxedo that split wide open. They were just trying
to do me a favor and *not* put my panties on display on live TV.
Whoops.

Regardless of my bikini bottom problems, my boy Kobe's rap debut didn't go over too well, and the single kinda got panned. In hindsight, we probably should have seen that coming: a super-athlete and a supermodel? Well, those two supers cancel each other out, and all you're left with is a serious lack of music cred. Sorry, Kobe. I wish I would have been seated at a different part of the theater at Teen Choice cuz I would have not had the opportunity to screw up your dream. Where was Lil' Kim when you needed her? Well, at least you didn't have to pay me, right?

Carolyn: Too many people stick to the path they know just because they're scared of failing if they go in a different direction. As much as I didn't think that Tyra's singing career was the right different direction, I was proud of her for taking risks and being fearless about it.

I'd been there before myself, and knew from experience that sometimes you just have to see for yourself whether or not something will work out.

When I was working at Cedars-Sinai Medical Center as a medical photographer, I was in a restaurant and got to talking to a woman who ran a portrait photography business. It was kind of like Glamour Shots, and she was about to open up a new studio in Los Angeles. "You should come work for us!" she said. "You're a photographer; you've done some fashion work! You could be a store manager! We'll put you in charge."

I had some experience shooting fashion lookbooks and head-shots for actors and models, so this portrait business seemed like a great way for me to try something new.

I walked out of there thinking, "Hmmm, store manager?"

I liked this idea, but no one else did.

"Carolyn, are you sure?" my friend Jackie asked. "You'd have to work with people in the mall. It'd be a lot of customer service, and I don't think you'd like that."

"What does Jackie know?" I thought, even though she and I had been best friends since we were fourteen and she always knew me better than I knew myself.

So I quit my great job as director of the medical media department at the hospital and headed to the mall.

Jackie was right—I did not like customer service. People complained all day long! They didn't like their makeup. Or they liked their makeup but hated their photos. One woman even ran right out the store without paying, and the employees looked at me like, "Aren't you the manager? Go chase that picture-pay-ditcher down!"

"Hmm," I thought, as I watched the woman's backside disappear past the food court. "Run, Forrest, run!"

Maybe this wasn't my dream job after all. . . .

I dusted myself off, polished my résumé again, and went and got a new job. Specifically, a new old job—I went right back to being the head medical photographer at Cedars-Sinai.

I walked back in there on my second first day with my head held high.

There ain't no shame in my failing game.

👁 👁 *Tyra:* OK, when I talk about how bad I was at singing, I'm overstating it a bit. I don't think droves of people would have been booing me offstage—they just wouldn't have been buying tickets to the next show. I knew about harmony and melody, and I was actually a pretty more-than-decent

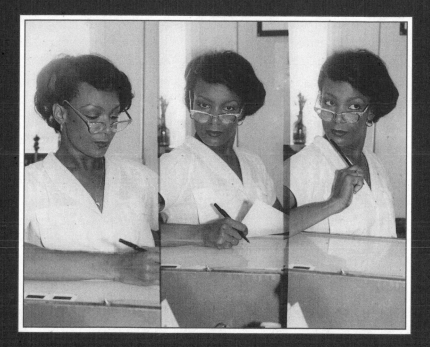

I know all you kids don't know what that is, but I was looking at slides there!
This was how we used to review pictures before the smartphone!

songwriter. Sometimes, I could even pass for a pretty more-than-decent singer if you caught me in just the right moment.

For example, when I got on the phone with Pharrell, we were vibing immediately. "I want to hear you sing," he said.

"Great!" I was so excited. "When do you want to meet up?"

"No," he said, "right now. I want to hear you sing right now. On the phone."

Oh, shoot . . . But no big deal. I reached deep down, pulled it together, and belted out a Brandy song, because I loved me some Brandy, and since I wasn't looking right at him, I could just pretend Pharrell wasn't there and I was just singing along to some hold music from the cable company.

When I finished, he was actually impressed.

"Oh my God," he said. "You're not Whitney Houston, but you can carry a tune. Like, for real. Let's do this."

Yes! This was really happening. I was going to work with Pharrell!

Then I got in his studio and "phell" on my face.

Carolyn: I tried to get Tyra to sing like she wasn't a serious singer. "You need to have a voice that's affected," I told her.

"What does that mean, Ma?"

"You know, like high-pitched, nasal, and cute. And maybe, sometimes, you talk instead of sing. Let's focus on how you're going to come across onstage. More emphasis on performing," I said, "and less emphasis on singing."

👁 👁 *Tyra:* I was a nervous mess when I got in the studio with Pharrell. He had a backup singer there, but soon it was more like she was there to sing the lead and I was supposed to provide background vocals for her. Pharrell (and most music producers) works with all kinds of people in the waiting room and studio, and in that room alone, there were probably more people than had ever heard me sing before in my entire life. I was sure that each and every one of them was laughing at me between takes.

Also, singing to Pharrell on the phone? No problem. Singing to his face? That was a whole different story. Plus he's gorgeous (that skin that looks like butterscotch satin and those Marcona almond–shaped eyes), so that didn't help. So let's just say I was far from feeling Happy. (See what I did there?) Anyway, the song he had for me was called "Playboy."

I can remember the lyrics and melody like it was yesterday:

Playboy
We gone have some big fun tonight
Playboy
And if it feels good
Then please don't pay attention
Let's just ride
Playboy

As I sing the song now as I am writing this, I sound pretty good. I'm breathing properly, holding the notes, adding a little vibrato, and doing a few vocal tricks. That's because Pharrell is not in front of me. This lets me know I needed the show *The Voice* to exist back then. I can imagine facing away from the singing star mentors and just belting "Playboy" at the top of my lungs and killing it. And then Pharrell would hit his buzzer, his big red chair would turn around, and he'd be like, "OMG! It's TyTy! What up, girl! Let's go to the studio now and lay this club banger down!"

Needless to say, that day in Pharrell's studio was a complete disaster. And "Playboy" never saw the light of day. Cue sad-face emoji.

Carolyn: We later went and met with David Foster, who'd worked with people like Michael Jackson and Céline Dion. He's talking about Tyra's stage presence and how if she can bring what she has on the runway to her songs, then she's gonna be a superstar. The whole time, my stomach is flip-flopping.

Then he gets up and goes over to his piano. He sits down and taps out some notes. "OK, Ms. Tyra, sing for me."

Tyra looks like she just swallowed a bug. "You mean now?"

"Yeah, now," he says with a smile. "Give me the money note."

"Mr. Foster!" Tyra says. "I can't do that."

"Sure you can," he says, his fingers dancing up and down the keys like he's done this a million times before, because he probably has. "Just blast it! Let it out! Give it to me!"

Tyra won't do it. Can't do it. So David has an idea. "Tyra, I will create a song for you, and you can come back and sing it in my Malibu studio," he offers. "Maybe you'll be more comfy in a booth."

Oh, Lord. Here we go again.

Tyra: To save a lot of time, let's just say the Foster session was similar to Pharrell's, minus about ten people. However, I did finish the song. It went something like this:

Our first kiss won't be the last . . .
And la la la la la la la (can't remember this part)
And good things come to those who have to wait.

It was kind of an innocent song. But my voice was kinda guilty. Guilty of being kinda talentless. David sweetly passed on making me his mega pop star of the world. But did that stop me? Sadly, no.

Carolyn: Mr. "Hitmaker" Foster was a class act. He had high hopes for Ty but was so gracious with his no. And for being so kind and gentle with my baby, I thank him. Tyra had a house in Orlando, and we would spend lots of time there, especially since it was so close to Disney World and Tyra was obsessed with the place. We would sit on the porch of her house on the lake and hear the bullfrogs croaking and watch the Disney fireworks go off every night at nine o'clock on the dot. She started to spend more and more time in Orlando so she could work on her music with leading music industry peeps based there, and she even got signed to Britney Spears's and 'NSync's music manager's company. She got to working with a few songwriters and producers down there, and I knew I hated the music industry when I realized that they thought it was totally acceptable to schedule meetings for midnight or one o'clock in the morning.

The area where Tyra lived was so rural that there weren't even streetlights, and it backed up to a nature preserve that was home to all kinds of critters that made your skin crawl. So there we were, driving into the night on these pitch-black streets so Tyra could record her demo, just hoping we didn't hit an alligator or wild boar along the way.

👁 👁 *Tyra:* In Orlando, I had worked a lot with a singer-songwriter named Billy Lawrence, and when I was in the studio with Billy, I was fine. She was my homegirl and I sang my heart out to her. I guess I felt safe because we hung out all the time chilling and eating at places like Joe's Crab Shack and Shoney's, so there was no pressure. I knew she was gonna help me out a bit (a lot) and Auto-Tune the crap out of my voice, but I didn't care; I was having fun with my buddy.

Wyclef was another story altogether. I was introduced to him by some friends, and he was warm and sweet and did his best to make me feel comfortable. But once I entered his NYC vocal booth, I again got so nervous—I was in the studio with Mr. Fugees!—and felt like I didn't have air in my lungs. The song he wrote for me was called "Why Does it Hurt So Bad?" I could barely eke out a squeak. And that hurt. So bad.

Eventually, I got in the studio with major music producer Rodney Jerkins. I was ecstatic. He was the man responsible for Brandy's signature sound! With Rodney, I gotta admit, I sounded hella good. To this day, I don't know how he got the vocals out of me that he did. I think a big part of it was the magical touch of his vocal producer, LaShawn Daniels. LaShawn told me that when I sang, I enunciated too much. I'd pronounce every single syllable, which he said made me sound like a stiff, proper lady with a stick up her butt—and no one wanted to hear a proper lady sing on pop radio. LaShawn coached me to sing with the smooth sound of where I was from: Inglewood, baby! He was a master. He taught me to write down all the lyrics of every song in phonetic slang. If you looked at the paper, it looked like I was slightly illiterate, but when they played it back to me, it sounded so good. "I love you so let me see what you are working with" became "Ah luhyoo suhlemme see wuhchoo werkinnwit"—it sounded so fly! It sounded unbelievable—I was like, "Wait a second, is that *me* on that track?" Plus, I did *all* my background vocals on every song!

Rodney was a friggin' genius! I ended up doing about ten songs with him and his Darkchild crew, and I felt like it was time. Time to go public.

Carolyn: Tyra had the grand idea to use *America's Next Top Model*'s power platform to launch this friggin' music career! Hold on to ya seats. We're getting close to that concrete wall!

Tyra: Besides, the public had been hearing me sing for years on *America's Next Top Model*. They just didn't know it. All those na-na-na-na-nas on the theme song from cycle 1 to more than twenty cycles later? That's your girl. Yeah, it's me!

I had been in the studio with the *Top Model* music producers when they were composing it, and I got in the booth to show them what I wanted. "We need a girl singer who can do these na-na-na-nas just like this," I said. I sang it, and they looked at each other, then looked back at me.

"Uh, you're here. Why don't we just have you do it?"

So I did, and people loved that theme song. That was proof that I had something, right? (The network replaced the "na-na-na" theme song in cycle 23, but when I came back to the show for 24, I rallied hard to pepper them back in.)

I wanted to debut with a mid-tempo jam called "Drivin' Me Crazy" to really show the people what I could do. But Rodney is the expert. He picked a song called "Shake Ya Body."

So, yes, we shot a video for it. On *Top Model* cycle 2. I have to

This was the actual CD from my big musical debut "Shake Ya Body." UPN printed a bunch of them as a promo (should I apologize to them as well?).

tell you, to this day, I still think that video was slammin'! The final six girls from that cycle all had starring roles. We shot some of it in front of a massive waterfall that the world didn't know was really located in an NYC Chinese tchotchke shop, though you would never know, because it looked like we pulled out all the stops. It looked like it cost a legitimate $300,000 (the price for nice videos at that time), even though we only spent $30,000 (the price of a photo shoot).

We shot the whole episode and dedicated it to the making and world premiere of that video, and it finally aired on *Top Model* months later. Now, get this: It was the highest-rated episode we'd ever had (still is to this day, actually. Can you believe it?). That was major! I got beyond excited.

"The people want me to sing!" said the devil on my shoulder.

"But do they really?" said the angel on the other, a.k.a. Mama.

And that got me thinking. . . .

I wondered, "Did people tune in en masse because they wanted to see me sing, or because they were hoping for a car crash?"

Still, I was gonna give singing one more go for the thing I loved the most: Disney.

Carolyn: Oh gosh, did that girl love Disney! When she was a child, we had to keep any Disney trips a secret, because if Tyra knew about them too far in advance, she'd get so excited that she wouldn't sleep for weeks.

Going to Disney was always an ordeal: You parked in Dumbo F95, which must stand for "95 miles to the ticket window," and then spent a month's wages on admission. ("Don't worry," I'd whisper to my husband as we forked over the cash. "We can always sell the car as soon as we get home.")

But it was worth it just to see Tyra so happy. As soon as she got through those gates, it was as if she had entered a magical, transformative world. Her whole demeanor changed. She didn't walk but skipped everywhere, talked in the voices and accents of

Stills from the "Shake Ya Body" video that premiered on *Top Model* cycle 2.
I still think this video was bangin'!

all the characters she came across, and scarfed down all the ice cream bars, caveman-size drumsticks, and churros she could get her hands on. And this was pre-FastPass, but it didn't matter how long those damned lines were; she was in heaven!

Tyra: I can't really overstate how much I love Disney. Saying "I loooooooooooooooooooooove Disney" gets close but still doesn't cut it because all those extra *o*'s don't reflect just how much of an influence it has had on me. We went as a family when my parents were married, but when they separated, my pop's divorced-dad guilt kicked in and he would take me to Disneyland. All. The. Time. Those multiple trips got me obsessed with immersive experiences and the power of a strong, positive brand. Sound, sight, taste, touch, smell. Disney didn't just entertain—it downright surprised, delighted, and dazzled all my senses!

The one bummer for me, though, was the whole princess thing. I mean, look at the Disney princesses of the 1980s. I looked nothing like Sleeping Beauty, Snow White, or Cinderella. And because of that, I knew I could never grow up and play a part in their famous Main Street Electrical Parade. They were all white, and not just Caucasian, but never-seen-the-sun-or-even-a-bronzer-brush alabaster.

While most kids left Disney with huge smiles on their faces, I was always on the verge of tears when we'd walk away from that spectacular electrical parade at the end of the night. "I can't be a princess, Daddy! I can't be on top of the float," I'd sob, "I have to be one of the dancing ladies on the ground."

So when Disney announced that they were doing *The Princess and the Frog*, and Princess Tiana was black, I damn near leapt off my lily pad.

"Oh my God!" I screamed, to any- and everyone who would listen. "I can be *this* princess! She's black. She's from Louisiana—I can do accents! I can sound younger! I was made to be a cartoon character."

Through all my yapping, I finally got an audition. And I killed it. Killed it enough to get a callback, which was where I really let loose. I did my lines to a T, and then when they wanted ad-libs, I was pulling out every Southern trick in my book. "You bess bring dem beignets ova here, boy," and "Dat swamp be fulla gaytas. I ain't goin' in dere." (LaShawn would have been proud.) Then when they wanted me to play the frog Tiana turns into, I was rib-biting all over the place like I'd just swallowed a teacup of tad-poles. I really went for it, and they were really impressed. "Wow, you're really good, Tiana!" said one of the casting directors. "OMG! He called me the character's name!" I shrieked in my head. I was flyin' high.

I knew it was in the bag when they offered to take me on a tour of the animation studio, and I was happier than I'd been since waiting an hour and a half for Space Mountain.

There were different renderings of Tiana and the frog all throughout the animation studio, some done on computers, some done by hand, some with short legs, some with long. There was the town where the story took place and even a drawing of Tiana's mom right next to a photo of Oprah! I felt like I was getting a real peek behind the scenes. "Oh my God," I thought. "They're doing this because they want me to see what my character is going to look like. I bet they're analyzing me so that the frog has some of my features? You know they like the animated animals to some-times kinda look like the real people playing them. . . ."

Everyone is coming up to me to introduce themselves, and we're all laughing, getting to know each other, and talking about how great my accent was and how strong I ribbited in the audition. I was having so much fun that I wasn't paying attention to where we were going. Until we ended up at a piano.

I saw it, and all I thought was "Oh cool, they've got a piano. This place has everything." Yeah, it still wasn't hitting me. I was still on my Disney cloud.

Then someone introduced me to the pianist. "Tyra, pick a song, any Disney song," he said.

"Um, what?"

Smiling faces surrounded me. "We just want to hear you sing," someone said. "So go ahead, whenever you're ready."

"Why do I have to sing?" I thought. "Did Cameron Diaz sing in *Shrek*? Can't someone else do the songs?"

Finally, I was able to buy myself some time. They still wanted me to sing, but they were going to let me prepare something for them and sing it later. I rushed out of there determined not to let my Disney princess dreams die.

Carolyn: Tyra was so, so happy when she was in the megahit Disney TV movie *Life-Size*. Girls around the world are obsessed with the doll-come-to-life character she played, Eve. But she really, really wanted to get the part of the Frog Princess. This was the time Tyra's overly enunciating, Broadway-style singing would have been spot-on, and she could sound so sweet and youthful. Her voice has always sounded much younger than she is. Besides, it would have made up for all those times I had to drag a crying little girl back to Dumbo F95 at the end of the Electrical Parade.

👁 👁 *Tyra:* Back at my house, I was trying. I was singing "Someday My Prince Will Come" and "I'm Wishing," and I was trying to get all those "ah-aha-aha" trills . . . and I was failing. Big-time. I call up my friend, superproducer and recording artist Kenneth Edmonds, a.k.a. Babyface, and almost cried to him about it. "They want me to sing and I want to impress them—what do I do?"

He told me to calm down and come to his studio. When I got there, he'd written a whole damn song for me to sing, about a girl and a frog in New Orleans. It had this sweet, swamplike, laid-back vibe to it, but it was still quintessentially Disney princess. It was bananas. To be clear, bananas to me means *amazing!* He kept humming and singing it to me, and trying to get me to sing it back with a full and strong voice. I just couldn't get it right, no matter how much I practiced.

"OK, so I'm totally incapable of singing your genius of a song," I said. "But you wrote an original Disney song for me in the span of a few hours and that's beyond dope; you should send it to them!" I don't think he ever submitted the song, but he should have. Did I say it was bananas?

I kept trying and trying different songs, and working with my vocal coach, until I was finally able to lay down that famed Pocahontas song, "Colors of the Wind" (the movie version, not the silky, soulful Vanessa Williams one—which I still loved, too), and I sent it to Disney. My fingers were crossed and I was holding my breath and turning blue. Then I got the phone call of phone calls. It was down to me and two other voices—both of whom were singers. One was a very famous singer from *American Idol* and a Dreamgirl. The other was also a Dreamgirl. Two Dreamgirls. Real singers. Dammit. But still, I was hopeful—those girls could sing, but what if they couldn't ribbit? And certainly, they couldn't want it as badly as I did, right? I practically came out of the womb wearing mouse ears—I was born to play this role.

I was so excited, I didn't sleep while I waited for the call. Every time the phone started ringing, I'd race across the room, vault the couch, and swing from the chandelier to answer it on the second ring. "Hello, Disney?" I'd breathlessly say into the receiver.

"No, um, it's the dry cleaner?" the voice on the other end would say. "Your shirts are ready."

"Ribbit."

"What?"

"Never mind. Thank you."

Finally, I got the call.

I held my breath while they told me the news I had never hoped for: Princess Tiana would be played by Anika Noni Rose. A real Dreamgirl.

My dream was over. Done. Was not gonna happen. I was devastated. Did this mean I had put all those lily pads in the pool for nothing? "Can't they just get Anika to do the songs and I'll be the acting voice?" I asked. I was OK with sharing! I had my agent call and call and call until finally she said, "Tyra, it's done. They're moving on, and you should, too."

Not long after I realized I wasn't going to be the princess, or even the frog, I was having lunch with my music manager, Benny Medina. Benny was the third music manager I'd had. Three managers, still no album. But I was hopeful. Benny had worked with J.Lo, so if he could help her become a pop star, maybe he could do it for me. "Tyra, I just want to check in and make sure I'm doing my job to your satisfaction," he said as I scarfed down my Caesar salad. "I want you to be happy and on the right path. So humor me: Imagine that you're walking into this restaurant a year from now. What do you want all these important people to think when they see Tyra Banks come through that door?"

We were at the Ivy, one of the most industry- and celebrity-heavy restaurants in L.A. As I looked around, I could see people who were super influential in fashion, film, TV, music, and business. Yeah, I knew that they were the "important" people, but I realized they weren't the main people I wanted to impress. In fact, in that moment, it hit me. I wanted to do more than just impress people. I wanted to connect with people. Deeply.

"I want people to feel power when I walk in," I told Benny. "But not the power that most people understand. Power doesn't just come from money and success; I think true power comes from being someone who speaks up about things that matter and works to make crappy things they see in the world better. I want to be a force for positive change. I want to make people feel better about themselves and show them that they're not alone."

Benny smiled and took a sip of his iced tea.

"Then why the hell aren't you doing a talk show?" he said.

In that moment, something in my brain clicked in a way it hadn't since I'd first had the idea for *Top Model*, standing in my kitchen in my underwear. "You can model, do *Top Model*, your music, and do a talk show . . ." he continued.

I nodded, but inside, I had already made up my mind.

Mama always said that in addition to having tunnel vision and focus, you need to have time to sit and do nothing so you can hear what your next moves should be to reach the pinnacle of success. Well, it was time I started listening.

A couple of days later, Benny received a phone call from me.

"Hi, Benny. I want to stop singing."

"What?"

"Yep. I'm going to put all of my energy into creating a kick-ass, game-changing talk show."

ALL APOLOGIES

Real women know when to say sorry. So, here I go: **Kobe:** I messed up your solo rap debut. **Pharrell/ Wyclef:** I wasted your time. **Benny:** You spent countless hours working with me on my singing strategy when you could have been spending more time with J.Lo. **David Foster:** Sorry for keeping you tied up in your Malibu studio when you could have been hanging with your beautiful future supermodel family and watching the sunset. **Babyface:** You wrote that song for me when you coulda been working on another hit for Whitney Houston! **Disney:** Well, ummmm . . . it's never too late. Ha!

Carolyn: I think your gut instinct is usually the right one. With Tyra, I think she always knew she wasn't supposed to be a singer, but she's not a quitter, so it took her a while to let that mic drop without picking it up again. When she finally did hit the brakes on her singing career, and called to tell me she was done, I did a secret happy dance. I could finally take a full breath again after all those months of biting my tongue and gritting my teeth every time someone asked her for the money note.

Tyra wasn't meant to be the next Katy Perry or J.Lo. But the girl could talk and had a gift for helping people see the inner and outer beauty they couldn't see in themselves.

👁️🗨️ 👁️🗨️ *Tyra:* I do think I was talented when it came to music. My talents just didn't lie on the mic. I was more of a behind-the-scenes girl: I wrote the theme song to the short-lived *FABLife* talk show and coproduced all the *Top Model* remixes. In my time, I think I wrote some damned good songs, if I do say so myself.

I teamed up with Big Bert (a producer who was dating Brandy at the time) to write a song called "Beautiful Girl." He had made this gorgeous melody, and we sat up in the studio until the wee hours of the morning, eating crab and garlic noodles from one of my fave spots, Crustacean, while he played it on a loop and I wrote the lyrics. It was all about how women should cherish the beauty of their soul and resist the pressure to be perfect (a theme that should sound familiar to you by the end of this book). I still think the world needs to hear this! Just not with me singing. With someone like Rihanna. Or maybe like . . . I don't know . . . Rihanna? So, what you think, world (Rihanna)? Should we put it out there? (Hey, Rihanna, DM me, girl. You won't be disappointed.)

But when I started preproduction of my talk show, I went all in. I put those singing dreams so far up on the shelf that I woulda needed a hundred-foot stepladder to get them down again. I was told that 90 percent of talk shows failed before the first season even wrapped. If I wanted my show to succeed, I needed to live it and breathe it. So I moved out of my huge Beverly Hills house into a tiny apartment across the street from the talk show studio.

Shortly after that, my idol and hero, Oprah, threw her famous three-days-long Legends Ball at her sprawling home in Montecito, California. She invited and celebrated women like Coretta Scott King, Maya Angelou, and Naomi Sims as the legends, and also included what she referred to as "young'uns," legends of the future. When I opened the most beautifully crafted and illustri-ous invitation I have ever received in the mail and saw that Ms. Winfrey considered me a young'un, I was speechless. To be rec-ognized by Oprah and to be surrounded by such incredible women was one of the most awe-inspiring experiences of my life. At the dreamlike luncheon on the first day, Oprah had this new singer she'd discovered perform, and he was just wonderful. "John Legend?" I remember thinking. "His voice is amazing! I'll have to remember that name in case he gets big."

Day two was a white-tie ball with a black-and-white dress code (you had to wear black or white—Oprah laid down that law), and there's Toni Morrison over here and Rosa Parks over there, and I'm intimidated just to be standing in the same room with all these, well, living legends. Oprah was the only person who wore red, and she looked like a rare, beautiful ruby fluttering throughout the party, never resting, constantly producing to make sure everything was running on point. "Oh my God, you look like a princess," she said when I entered the ballroom as she hugged me. "You know what? Better yet, a queen." If I couldn't be a Disney princess, being an Oprah queen was the next best thing. No, it was better.

At the ball, this young senator gave an incredible speech, with-out even reading anything off a teleprompter, and there was hardly a dry eye in the place because he was speaking so raw, so real, and from the heart. I can be a little shy in places like this, and after dinner, my wacky friend dragged me out of my chair to dance and work the room. Eventually, we made our way over to the senator, and my buddy was being her fun, wild self and talking to him like she'd known him her entire life—she may have dropped a few expletives here and there. She had me blushing through my bronzer—oh my God, girl, this man is important!—and when she walked away, I apologized to him in case she'd offended him.

"What, you think I've never heard those words before?" he said with a laugh. He was the nicest, realest politician I'd ever met.

"Huh," I thought as I walked away from our conversation. "Barack Obama. I better remember that name, too."

The closing event of the weekend was a Sunday brunch, and for this, we were allowed to bring a date. I, of course, brought my date for life: my mama. Across all her sprawling acres, Oprah had set up picnic tables full of barbecue and other tasty tidbits, but the highlight came before the food: a gospel revival concert helmed by BeBe Winans (who I am low-key obsessed with. His voice is one of my all-time faves!). At some point, they started singing a classic gospel song called "Changed," and it was clear that everybody knew the words.

BeBe started passing the mic.

He passed it to Shirley Caesar, who tore it up. "He changed me!" she sang at the top of her lungs. Then Dionne Warwick was on deck. Whew, yes, child! Then Yolanda Adams. Sang, girl, sang! As Usher looked on, the mic then went to Chaka Khan—*Let me rock you, let me rock you, Chaka Khan*! Gladys Knight then took control and put some *Pip* in all our steps. Valerie Simpson did her thing while her husband cheered her on, and Patti LaBelle took us home, baby! Mama was sitting next to me, crying and clapping along and having the time of her life.

That is when something dawned on me. Something horrible.

"Mama, oh my God," I said as soon as the song was over. "If I had a hit song on the radio right now, they would have passed that mic to me!"

Carolyn: If they would have passed the mic to Tyra, I would have done what any good mother would do: created a distraction and told her ass to run.

Tyra: That moment there with my mom, in the presence of my idol Oprah and so many other greats, was the moment when everything was so clear to me. I realized just how strong one could be if they focused on their strengths. Yes, we all have dreams and fantasies and desires, and those are all worth exploring—but I now see that we shouldn't blindly force it. Listen to your gut, because it usually knows what's up.

The downside of being really driven is that sometimes you keep your foot on the gas even when you're going in the wrong direction, but I don't regret all that time (six years) and money (thousands upon thousands) I spent trying to make a singing career happen. That time helped me identify my weaknesses. Knowing my weaknesses helped me identify my strengths. I had to learn to tell the difference between a dream and a calling, and focus my life on following the calling, not chasing the dream. Just because I couldn't sing didn't mean I couldn't use my voice for good.

Carolyn: "Mm-hmm, baby," I told Tyra after that "Changed" song with the powerful voices wrapped up. "I'm so happy you *changed* your mind. You are now focused on your gift, which is giving people opportunities they never thought they could ever have had. And I think for that, for your talking voice and power, one day when you're old and gray—and you will not dye your hair—for all that you did, you, too, will be called a legend."

HAPPILY EVER AFTER

👁 👁 *Tyra:* When *The Princess and the Frog* came out, I had a couple of the cutest little girls on my (two-time best show Emmy-winning—yep, it was my calling) talk show. The gist was that they couldn't afford to go to the movie, so we surprised them by taking their families on a plane to Disney World to see the movie and to meet Princess Tiana. At the amusement park, the girls were so excited and screaming and crying, and hugging Tiana like her princess powers would rub off on them if they got close enough.

I have to admit, for a second I looked at that princess and thought, "That coulda been me." But then I snapped right back to reality. I was actually glad it wasn't, because Tiana for me was never meant to be.

But Disney, if you ever need a princess who raps . . . well, holla at ya girl. I even got a ninth-grade rhyme I know by heart.

YOU'RE STILL IN THE RUNNING

👁 👁 *Tyra:* This book is almost done (yay, you!), but the love doesn't stop. Our love continues to pour down on you. That doesn't mean it's always going to be something you want to hear. Nope—it will be what you *need* to hear. And you might not like it all that much.

Carolyn: You might not like *us* all that much, but that's OK. We got that tough love for you, baby. Sometimes tough love hurts, especially when you're balancing both of us on your shoulders every darn day.

But that's what makes you stronger. That's what makes you grow.

Y'know?

Tyra: I live in all mirrors you look into, reminding you that you are fierce, flawsome, and ferocious.

Carolyn: I am the cheerleader out there shaking my pom-poms and urging you on when you feel it's too hard to keep on keepin' on.

Tyra: I am your ride-or-die chick who gives your self-doubt a dropkick and a bitch slap every time its dirty little butt sneaks into your head.

Carolyn: I am that (extra) momma (you never knew you had) who always has your back and will shake you, wake you, but never break you.

👁 👁 *Tyra:* I am your sister (from another mister) who resides in every hallway you encounter, encouraging you to work it like a runway.

So yeah, sometimes we're here to grab you by the shoulders and shake some sense into you, and sometimes we're here to hold your hand and rub your shoulders 'cause we know what you're going through.

And be warned: Just 'cause this is the end of the book, it doesn't mean it's the end of our story or yours. It's just the beginning.

Why?

Cuz this is the kind of book where it's almost over and you get kinda sad. Cuz you want it to go on and on and on. It's like your BFF. So you know what? We may be back in book two with more "for real" talk, a new set of eight words to watch out for (oh yeah, and they're bananas), crazier stories, TMI, OMG truth bombs, and more reminders that beauty is in the Smize of the beholder.

When you kick perfection to the curb once and for all and embrace your beauty, your booty, and your whole flawsome self, ain't nobody gonna be shouting love for you louder than us.

So whether you're just starting your period, it's about to end for good, or your daughter's just started flowing . . . we're rooting for you!

Or when you drop the mic because you know that whatever you've chosen to do may not be your calling and it's time to focus on your true gifts . . . we're rooting for you!

And when you refuse to change just for other people and accept that an ass that is fat or flat is all that . . . we're rooting for you!

Or when someone whispers those eight words in your ear and you think, "Oh, hell no!" (Or maybe "Oh, hell yes!") . . . we're rooting for you!

We're ~~all~~ both rooting for you!

And remember, perfect is boring. But you, my dear, ain't boring. Not one bit.

So go forth, you crazy, amazing, strong, imperfect human being, and make all your fiercest dreams comes true, boo.

Love, TyTy and Mama Carolyn

JOIN OUR MOVEMENT!

Mothers and daughters, fathers and sons, and everyone in between—we want you! As you just experienced first-hand, this book is real and raw. We stripped down to the cold, hard, messy truth, and we want you to do the same.

Can you handle your *own* truth? That truth that makes you a little, or a lotta umcomfy . . . makes you squirm in your seat.

We are here to help you.

Share your imperfect moments at PerfectIsBoring .com or on social media with #PerfectIsBoring. You can do it. We know you can!

We also get crazy IRL, so be sure to check the website for *Perfect Is Boring* events coming to a town near you. Bring your best Smize, boo, but leave your inhibitions at the door. And we may call you up to take the floor, so be ready to roar.

ACKNOWLEDGMENTS

Carolyn & Tyra:

Devin Banks

Genius son and boisterous bro,

Lived these crazy stories up close, fo' sho'.

Don Banks

I'll always be your crazy baby girl

And you're the best daddy in the whole crazy world.

Carolyn:

Benjamin McAdoo III

For the persistent pep talks, patience, and pet care

And the real, raw honesty—yeah, you really went there!

Donna Givens

Through thick and thin booties, and lotsa hard times,

Your solid support scrubbed away my life's grime.

Tyra:

Kenya Barris

My buddy since six, and you now got six babies!

I forgive you for stealing my dictionary (maybes).

Nancy Josephson

Major supporter with runway-ready style

Your love and support are felt here, and for miles.

Carolyn & Tyra:

Mel Berger

Bold book agent full of backing and belief

This book's fearless leader and commander in chief.

Roy Campbell

Our fashion friend family never doubted our glory,

His dedicated work built the foundation of this story.

Tyra:

Ricky Hutchinson

The anything and everything go-to guy

Who tracked down all photos and never questioned why.

Carolyn & Tyra:

Kate Williams

The world's best wordsmith playmate

Straight-up kept our voices straight.

Carolyn:

Aya & Fredo

For the missed doggie walks while Mama pounded computer keys

I'll make it up with some bacon doggie treats.

Tyra:

Sara Carder and everyone at TarcherPerigee

For believing in us and our crazy story

And helping us escape that hurry-up-we-need-to-make-this-release purgatory.

Carolyn & Tyra:

Jackie Prescod—no rhyming here . . .

My BFF who never left my side. Until she did . . . way too soon. My eyes to the sky, Jackie . . . I miss you.

—Carolyn

I miss you, too, Aunt Jackie. I can still hear your laugh. And I still wear your mint green earrings.

—Tyra

PHOTO CREDITS

ABOUT THE AUTHORS

Tyra Banks is the supermodel, super entrepreneur, and super CEO of our time. As an original Victoria's Secret Angel, the first African American model to be featured on the cover of the *Sports Illustrated* swimsuit edition, and the creator/executive producer of one of the longest-running competition shows, *America's Next Top Model*, Tyra has made it her life's mission to expand the definition of beauty and to empower women worldwide. In 2012, she graduated from the Owner/President Management program at Harvard Business School, and now teaches personal branding at Stanford University's Business School. She has been listed twice among *Time* magazine's "100 Most Influential People in the World" and is also the two-time daytime Emmy Award–winning host of the hit show *America's Got Talent*. She adores her son, the color yellow, and barbecue, and is an inventor of many terms, including "Smize" (smile with your eyes), "flawsome" (flaws are awesome), and "H2T" (head to toe), and dreams up new ones daily.

Carolyn London, a native of Los Angeles, California, is a retired professional photographer, mother to Tyra and her brother, Devin, and the CEO emeritus of the Tyra Banks Company and cofounder of the TZONE Foundation. She is the grandmother of five grandchildren and two great-grandchildren. She is an avid gardener (obsessed with succulents), dreams of being a master ceramic potter (but keeps on procrastinating on signing up for the next round of classes on the potter's wheel), and has the goose bump–inducing singing voice Tyra always wishes *she* had.